Uprooted and Replanted

Uprooted and Replanted

The Memoir of Helmut Heckscher
From Hamburg to the Kindertransport to America

Plus Reflections on the Life of
Catherine Bridget Heckscher, née Tancock

Compiled and Edited by Zahara Heckscher
With Assistance from Rachel Heckscher and David Spence

Helmut Heckscher

To order additional copies of this book, contact:
Xlibris
1-888-795-4274
www.Xlibris.com
Orders@Xlibris.com
546894

Contents

Introduction

Letter from Helmut Heckscher to his children

2007

Dear David, Joan, and Rachel,

For years I have thought to write an autobiography before I die or before I lose my memory. Even now, it often fails me. I regret that my parents, like most parents, did not leave a memoir of their lives, their hopes, successes, failures and disappointments. They might have been glad to talk about these things if I had asked them. But now it is too late.

For several reasons, I have so far shied away from writing an autobiography, or even this letter to you of my life, since "autobiography" seems a bit pompous. One reason is that I tend to procrastinate and defer writing to other easier, more entertaining, or more pressing tasks. Other difficulties, perhaps related, added to my hesitation. What voice should I adopt? A detached, benign, humorous point of view or a serious one? The view of the child as I was then, or the view of an eighty five year old, looking back? Then, too, like other memoirists, I have to decide what to select, and how much of myself I want to divulge. In writing about my parents, for instance, should I describe their shortcomings or, since they are dead and cannot defend themselves, should I withhold this criticism? Perhaps even more to the point, did they really fail as parents, or is it merely the way I perceive them?

I have no pearls of wisdom to convey to you, unless, unbeknownst to me, they are hidden in this account like pearls in a shell. I do not know the meaning of life and cannot tell you how to be happy or successful. Though

I don't have any answers, I will forge ahead as best as I can. Fortunately, since I have you as a captive audience, what I write need not be of universal interest. And if this letter is found hundreds of years from now, even what is mundane today might be important to historians.

There is still another reason for telling my story: I have heard that a drowning person will often see a flashback of his or her life. I hope that I will never experience such an exit. I prefer to write about my life in the comfort of my apartment.

Love from Dad (Helmut Heckscher)
Updated June, 2007

Introductory Note from Helmut's Daughter, Zahara Heckscher

May 31, 2017

When my father Helmut Heckscher passed away on May 21st, 2008, he left a draft of this memoir on his trusty old Mac computer. My sister Rachel, her husband Eric Olson, and I saved the chapters for future reference. Eight years later, I finally began the work to turn it into a book. I compiled the electronic copies, added some changes from hard copies he left, and included in the appendix reflections about the life of my mother and Helmut's wife, Catherine Bridget Heckscher, nee Tancock.

I am gratified to know that Helmut's grandchildren and others will have this book to learn about him – his journey from Germany to England as part of the *Kindertransport*; his subsequent immigration to the US via London during the Blitz; his experiences in the US and the Pacific after WW II; and his work as an inventor. I believe his story, as a refugee of the Holocaust who restarts his life in America, is remarkable.

Compiling and (lightly) editing this document turned out to have many joyful moments and surprises. I discovered quite a few things about my father I had not known, or had forgotten: His first university experience was at an internment camp for Germans in England, where he slept in a stable at a former racetrack. While in training as a member of the Signal Corps at Camp Crowder in Missouri, he spent weekends learning how to fly a plane. And after WWII, he served as a civilian in the US military in Japan, and was once assigned by the US government to carry bags of money across Japan... and left the bags on a train seat.

In addition, I came to a new appreciation of my father's distinctive writing style, with its thoughtful introspections, colorful vignettes, and entertaining digressions. He worked hard for over a decade to polish this work, taking memoir-writing classes, reading books about memoirs, and hiring editors. I would say he succeeded in writing a book that not only tells an interesting story, it tells the story with clear and engaging language, no small feat considering English was his second language.

This memoir allowed me to see Helmut as the complex person he was, not just as the father I experienced. In his letter above, he notes the difficulty he faced when deciding to write about a parent who has passed away. He asks "Should I describe their shortcomings or, since they are dead and cannot defend themselves, should I withhold this criticism?" I faced some similar challenges. Editing this memoir helped me find some understanding and healing, even while being astounded by some of his perspectives – especially his views of our life after our mother died and the gap between his experience of that time and mine. My feelings are softened when I reflect on the triple trauma Helmut experienced in his life: A family of origin that did not provide him with strong emotional skills, the ordeal of growing up as a Jew in Nazi Germany and being forced to flee his home, and the heartbreak of losing his wife to cancer in her prime, when we three were still young.

In this memoir, Helmut writes about all these difficulties in a straightforward way, without self-pity. Yet I know they affected him, and I believe they diminished his ability to be the kind of parent we wanted. I am comforted by knowing that David, Rachel, and I all turned out reasonably well; we all have worked hard in our own ways to heal ourselves and to try to pass healthier relationship skills on to the next generation. I also know we have all benefitted from many of the positive traits my father modeled, including a love of learning, an appreciation for nature, an inventive spirit, and a deep belief in social justice.

Helmut did not finish this memoir. Many sections are incomplete and significant parts of his life are missing entirely from his writing. In particular, there is a gap in the section from when he met Bridget (his wife, our mother) to when she died – a gap that includes all of the early years of our childhood. I talked to Dad about this gap when he was working on the memoir. I provided some suggestions that I thought might be helpful prompts. It seems that they were not helpful. My suggestions remain in the text as questions he never answered. He simply states of our early childhood: "These were the best years in my life." We all remember things differently. Dad was an honest man, and I believe that his words are the truth as he remembered it. Through my research to fill in some blanks and verify some facts, I connected with various helpful scholars in Germany, including Anke Hönnig of the Hamburg State Archive, and Professor Claudia Schnurmann of the University of Hamburg. I also had the pleasure of finding and communicating with writer Rosemary Mild, the granddaughter of Harry Bragarnick. As detailed in the memoir and appendix, Mr. Bragarnick, along with Rosa (Rose) Hoga, saved my grandparents from Hitler, and were responsible for Helmut coming to the United States. I deeply appreciate the assistance of the scholars, and the opportunity to renew the special bond between the Bragarnick and Heckscher families.

My edits on this document were mostly limited to copyediting for typos, commas, spaces, and the like, plus fixing footnotes and formatting, adding appendices and attachments, all with lots of help from the talented Aliyah Silver. I made some slight changes in the order of certain parts, and other light edits for clarity. Aliyah helped me transform the discombobulated drafts and primary documents into this book. She typed up the notes from friends at Bridget's memorial service – from documents kindly passed on to me after all these years from Martin Weil. I added footnotes, and tried to make it clear which notes were from me and which from Helmut. I left Helmut's sometimes meandering thoughts, occasionally nonstandard syntax, and his literary experiment with "Doubleman" in the last chapter.

Additional documents, including original copies of birth certificates and the like, are in the Helmut Heckscher files, as of this writing, located in my office. Helmut's other children, my brother David Spence, and sister Rachel Heckscher, may have additional documents. They both have been very supportive of my work on this project, assisted with the editing, and gave advice when I needed it. I thank them for the encouragement and contributions.

I am grateful that Helmut chose to write about his life, that we all might remember and learn from it, and that we might pass on this memories and experiences through the generations. In that spirit, I dedicate my work on this project to Helmut's grandchildren, who I love so dearly: Cecily, Henry, Phoebe, and Max.

With love,

Zahara Heckscher

Chapter 1

Origins of the Heckschers

The name Heckscher first appeared in the late 1500's in a Jewish shtetl near the small town of Hoexter in Eastern Germany. Shakespeare and Galileo were still young men then, and Newton was not yet born. The Heckschers were so-called Ashkenazi Jews who had come to Europe centuries ago from Palestine. (In contrast, the Sephardic Jews had come to North Germany from Spain to flee from the inquisition). Since they spoke Yiddish, there seems to be some evidence that some of them settled in or near Hoexter, which, according to the custom became the family name Heckscher.[1] Apparently at least some of them then moved to Hamburg. There, in 1589, an Ephraim Maier Heckscher was born.[2] From him, we and all other Heckschers can trace our ancestry. (I have an extensive genealogy dating from the 16th century to the present.)[3]

Inscriptions on tombstones in Hamburg and its suburbs, and other documents, show that until about 1800 all of the Heckschers were Orthodox Jews. The men were expected to study the Torah. Several became famous rabbis and Jewish communal leaders. However, all that changed after Napoleon invaded Germany in 1806. Suddenly, Jews were allowed to convert to Christianity and thus to escape prejudice and social and economic ostracism. Well-known converts of that period include the German poet, Heinrich Heine, England's Prime Minister, Benjamin Disraeli, and one Moritz Heckscher. The latter, after conversion in 1808 at age eleven, was baptized Johann Gustav Wilhelm Moritz Heckscher. He later became a Minister of Foreign Affairs. Holding this position would not have been possible if he had still been Jewish. (His son August immigrated to the US and became a noted philanthropist.)[4]

My Immediate Family

From family documents that my parents left me[5], I learned that my great-grandfather, Moses Meyer, was born in Hamburg in 1798 (son of Meyer Joseph Heckscher and Mine, nee Krushaber) and died in 1857. His wife, Claerchen (daughter of a teacher named Beer Israel and his wife Hitzel, nee Goldschmidt), was born in Schwerin (Silesia) in 1810 and died in 1886. They not only rejected the chance to convert, but, as shown in their 1833 marriage contract, remained Orthodox Jews. Their traditional marriage contract specified my grandmother's dowry, right down to "beds, bed sheets, linen, clothing, bonnets, caps, and underwear." It also included the stipulation that if she died before her husband, he had the duty, according to Jewish law, to marry her unmarried sister.

I don't know how long the strict adherence to Jewish law persisted in my family. My parents, for example, had lost all but the most superficial religious affiliation. As far as I know, they knew no Hebrew and paid only lip service to Judaism by going to a reformed temple on the High Holidays and by attending Passover dinners at homes of more observant friends. They saw to it that I had a Bar Mitzvah at the age of fourteen which, for me, was essentially an empty ceremony. But they were also proud, as am I, of those fellow Jews who have done much for humanity.

Moses Meier and Claerchen's son (my grandfather), Eduard, was born in Hamburg on September 28, 1836. In 1867 Eduard, then 31, inherited a cigar factory in Hamburg, which soon bore the name "Eduard Heckscher & Co." (This factory, according to my father, had been founded in 1822, perhaps by Moses Meyer Heckscher, my great-grandfather.) My grandmother, Johanna (Hannchen) Lippstadt, was born on March 22, 1846. She was the daughter of cattle trader Hirsch Lippstadt and Fanny, nee Susmann. In 1872, my grandparents Eduard and Johanna were married.

My father, Max Heckscher, was born in Hamburg in June, 1878.[6] He went to school at from Easter of 1884 to the Easter of 1894, when he graduated from a school known as the Holstentor at age 16. He then became an apprentice in a mercantile firm where he stayed 30 months as a traveling salesman. When he left the firm his employers wrote that he had "performed to our greatest satisfaction." He joined his father's cigar business and became a partner in 1907 at age 29. In 1911, he became the sole owner.

My grandmother, Johanna died on March 6, 1910. My father told me that my grandfather Eduard developed gangrene in his legs and that he procured ether for Eduard to ease his pain. Eduard died at age 78 on August 22, 1914, about three weeks after the start of World War I.

During the war my father joined the Sanitation Corps of the German army. He had always been fond of dogs and was assigned to a unit that trained dogs to find and help retrieve the wounded after the battles. I am sorry that he never talked to me about this phase in his life.

While traveling around the country as a salesman for my grandfather's tobacco company, my father met my mother, Friederike (Friedel) Leipziger, in Jauer [7] a small East German town where she and her older sister Else ("Miez") were born. My father proposed to her but she rejected him in favor of a second cousin. However, in 1917, three years into World War 1, my mother's previous engagement having broken up, my parents were married. She was then only 22; my father was already 39. The newlyweds moved into an apartment on the second floor of a rather posh apartment house at 12 Eppendorferlandstrasse, a main street in Eppendorf, a Hamburg suburb.

One of my father's sisters, Anna, whom I called "Tante Boebs," had married Albert Lippstadt who owned a small clothing factory in downtown Hamburg. Located on one of the floors of the Kloepper building[8], it employed about 20 workers, mostly female. During World War I, Albert became ill, perhaps with syphilis, and died in a sanatorium in 1918. The year before, Anna had asked my father to join her in managing the factory, as she had no business experience. In 1927, my father dissolved the tobacco company his father had founded.[9] Some time later he bought his sister's share of the clothing factory and became sole owner of what continued as "Albert Lippstadt and Co."

My father's other sister, Frieda, had married Willy Pintus and lived in Berlin. My father was not close to either of them and we saw them rarely. Unlike my parents, Anna remained in Germany after the outbreak of World War II. When the Nazis began to send Jews to concentration camps, she first tried to keep from being deported by becoming a patient in a Jewish hospital. When that ruse eventually failed, Anna committed suicide. Frieda died in a concentration camp in Riga.[10]

Chapter 2

My Beginnings and Childhood in Hamburg

I was born on September 18, 1921 in a Hospital in Eppendorf, an upscale suburb of Hamburg, the son of Max Heckscher and Friederike Heckscher, nee Leipziger. The event, alas, was not considered newsworthy, even in the local papers. Other events predominated that year, according to TIME magazine: Germany was to cough up 33 billion Marks for having started World War I, while in America, Warren Harding was sworn in as 29th president, Utah banned women's skirts more than 3" above the ankle, the average US income was $2,134, and the average life expectancy was 54.1 years. My parents, of course, rated me the most important event in 1921. They took me home and engaged a nanny, a young country girl, and a cook by the name of Rosa Hoga, who was to play a major role in our lives.

My mother had hoped for, and may have been disappointed with, my arrival.[11] (My feeding schedule and baby photos are in an appendix or files.) As a very small child, I visited my mother's parents at least once. They still lived in Jauer, Silesia, now in Poland, only about an hour's train ride from Berlin, but many hours from Hamburg. I got sick on the train, not from the motion but from the locomotive's acrid smoke. I've been told that while driving to their house from the train station in a horse cart over a cobblestoned road, I exclaimed, "Das ist so holperich" ("This is so bumpy"). My grandparents found this remark funny, coming as it did from a tiny city slicker used to the much smoother roads in his hometown.

A photo shows my mother's father Max Leipziger standing in front of his store where he brewed and sold whiskey and perhaps other alcoholic beverages. My grandmother's name was Henrietta Leipziger, nee Bacher. Soon after they were married, my parents moved from one apartment on the Eppendorferlandstrasse to another on the same block. A few days after the move, my absentminded father, having kept the keys to the old apartment, astounded the new tenants when they came home one evening and found him sitting in their living room.

A few years later we moved again, this time to a more modern fourth floor apartment at Haynstrasse 21, almost across the street from the old one. Both buildings were still there when I visited this area in 1993. The apartment consisted of a dining room, a living room, a kitchen and bathroom, two bedrooms, and a room for our cook after Rosa left, Henny.

Early Memories[12]

As a small boy in the 1920s, I was often taken to the factory where I was proudly displayed to the workers who stopped cutting and sewing pajamas and shirts to chat with me. We had to use an elevator called a *paternoster* to reach the factory floor. It had no doors. Like the Catholic prayer beads after which it was named, it moved without stopping, but so slowly that one could get on without risk. The cage ascended in one channel. At the top it went around a big wheel and descended in an adjacent channel. I always feared that if we accidentally passed the top floor, our cage would turn upside down and we would be dumped.

My parents were moderately well-to-do when I was small. Besides the cook, who I will describe later, we had a series of nannies, called *Kindermaedchen*, who lived with us until I went to school. This would be thought a luxury today; but then most German middle-class families had servants. With my mother at work, one or another of the nannies looked after me. Typically, she was a young country girl. I remember visiting one of them on her parents' farm. I must have become very fond of two of them, named Mariechen and Eila. My mother later told me that whenever she asked me if I loved her I would reply, "I only love Eila." I have often wondered since, whether our repartee was innocent banter, whether I meant to hurt her, or whether I'd really become more attached to these young women than to my mother. It must have been traumatic for me when these nannies were eventually dismissed or left on their own.

Once, my father bought a car. I suspect that my mother talked him into it. Since he didn't know how to drive he had to hire a chauffeur.[13] The chauffeur was separated from us by a glass window that slid aside, much like in today's taxis. We could only speak to him through a tube. After a few months, my father found the chauffeur had cheated on fuel and repair bills. My father fired him, then sold the car. After that we again relied on streetcars, subways and trains, or went on excursions with friends who had cars.

During the summer, my parents usually rented a cottage in Blankenese on the river Elbe, a short train ride from Hamburg[14]. Blankenese was a lovely village mostly of cottages built on a hillside that sloped down to a beach on the river. The Elbe there is quite wide; I should think a mile or so, and we would watch the large ocean liners gliding by on their way from the North Sea to Hamburg and back. In the mornings I went to a Kindergarten which I liked so much that I was often grumpy when my mother, often with her visiting sister Miez, picked me up for long walks in the afternoon. My mother and aunt talked grownup talk, and I trotted behind, terribly bored. On weekends my father joined us in Blankenese.

I remember trying to catch birds on the terrace of our Blankenese cottage. My parents and other grownups told me that one could easily catch a bird by putting salt on its tail. The humor of that advice was probably lost on me, and I spent many enjoyable hours trying to catch birds in this manner. I looked forward to a promised excursion to a village called Kranz, across the river from Blankenese, because I associated Kranz with *Kuchenkranz* (cake-ring). I was therefore dismayed and shed many tears when the village turned out to be just a village, bearing no resemblance to a delicious piece of cake.

Back in Hamburg, in the fall in time for school, my mother usually joined my father in his factory, a few hours after he left in the morning. I think my mother worked by choice, rather than from economic necessity. I have no idea what she did there. She also had a small business on the side. She bought inexpensive etchings, had them sprayed with an antiquing lacquer and then glued them to book covers, wastepaper baskets, and the like. She probably sold these to people she knew, rather than to stores.

My mother and her sister, Miez, attended a provincial school in Jauer where they were born and lived until they married. Even in her 60's, my mother could still recite the succession of Roman Emperors she had once learned by rote, a list of names ending with "-us": Tiberius, Claudius, Aurelius, Tacitus, Julianus. But it was their names she recalled, not their deeds. By contrast, Miez was better read, played the piano, and knew Italian. In their youth, they had complemented each other.

It was only when my mother's beauty faded that Miez, who was a bit plainer than she, began to outshine her sister. Perhaps in an effort to compete with Miez, my mother became overly assertive and self-righteous. I think that, especially in her later years, she would have been a happier woman had she not felt restricted by her gender. But when she died in the 1960's in the Midwest, the voices of women's liberation had hardly reached her.

As a boy, my father attended high school in Hamburg. His grades were middling and his education ended with his school days. He read the daily paper, but his conversation ranged little beyond the here and now. He had heard of Freud, but not read him. He said that Freud overvalued sex. He said, almost with pride, that he hated Bach.

Although my parents most likely tried to be good parents, like just about every parent, there was no Dr. Spock to guide them. On their own, they sometimes seemed to lack even common sense. Parents, for instance, have many options to deal with a naughty child. They can use love, force, or reason. My otherwise nonreligious parents chose a fourth way in my opinion, the worst of all. They quoted the fifth Commandment "Thou shalt honor thy father and thy mother." God himself had decreed this, and there was I, Helmut, defying God's word! Talk about guilt! Even worse, they read me a Grimm's fairy tale, probably the shortest, which I found in "Die Maerchen der Brueder Grimm." Translated (by me), it reads as follows:

The Obstinate Child

Once upon a time there was an obstinate child who did not do what its mother wanted. Therefore the dear God took a dislike of it and caused it to become ill so that no doctor could help it. Soon it was on its deathbed. After it was put in its grave and covered with earth, it happened that its little arm reached up. When its arm was put down and covered with fresh earth, it didn't help and its little arm continued to come up, so the mother herself had to go to the grave and hit the little arm with a whip. And when she had done this, the child pulled its arm down and only now had peace.

Its hidden message must have terrified me. But what is the message? That God favors parental cruelty of a child's obstinacy? I often think about the cruelty of my mother to tell me this story. But then, why had she remembered the story? Had her parents read it to her, selected from one of hundreds of other Grimm tales? And if they had, does that mitigate my mother's cruelty?

My mother seemed to think that the perfect man was strong, energetic, and scorned adversity. Perhaps she gained her ideas from movies or popular novels. In any case, my father was not such a man. He was soft-spoken, introverted, and worried a lot. This was not surprising, given the increasing threat from the Nazis and our uncertain future. I don't know if he loved my mother. If he did, I never saw signs of overt affection. My mother looked to me to fill this void, but seems to have forgotten that I was only a child and not a substitute for a husband. By frequently asking for, and even demanding my love, she made me dislike and fear her. This, of course, hurt her. She made tearful scenes and complained to my father. He always took her side and reproached me for making her cry. I wish he had been more impartial. But he told me a few years before he died that he thought all women were a little crazy, and that he had not expected anything more from her because she was a woman.

I learned to protect myself from these emotional entanglements by distancing myself from my parents. This protected me, but it also made me feel guilty for causing their unhappiness. My parents said I was cold and abnormal for not seeming to love them, while normal children loved their parents as a matter of course. When I easily took offence to criticism, they chided me for being overly sensitive. Perhaps they were right! But it seems to me now that to criticizing a small child for being oversensitive is like shouting at a child for being too shy, or scolding the child for crying. It's entirely counter-productive.

I still carry emotional scars from these early-life experiences. I am easily hurt by criticism and neglect and often retaliate quickly by withdrawing or by counterattack. The latter could be verbal or it could be a fantasy. I may think of ways to inconvenience or annoy the person who had caused my hurt. But these strategies have drawbacks: the criticism may have been just, and I might have profited from it. I may have imagined neglect when there was none, as when somebody neglected to return my telephone calls and I found later that he had been out of town. Even if my retaliation gives me some short-term satisfaction, it may be at the cost of losing a friend.

I was about six when I started elementary school at the Breitenfelder Strasse, close to home. The first day was marked in a traditional, festive way. Joined by their parents, the children walked to school carrying large, colorful cornucopias filled with candy. This custom made us look forward to our first day of school. It also gave us pride to be officially welcomed to the world of serious scholars.

One of my classmates was Karl, a squat, little fellow. He dressed poorly, probably in corduroys, and came from a working class family. Perhaps he even spoke Plattdeutsch at home. Plattdeutsch was a language, somewhat akin to Dutch, that was spoken by many workers in Hamburg at that time. Though I did not play with him after class, I greatly admired him. He was a salt-of-the-earth kind of kid; simple, perhaps, but honest and straightforward. He showed me that there were people outside the middle class world in which I lived. I think that my parents might have been dismayed had I brought him home because he was working class.

Henny, our cook after Rose Hoga left, had a small room in our apartment. Henny was plain and had a harelip. Looking back, I find it strange that I don't remember ever talking to her, except for conventional greetings. Henny was a good cook. When she prepared our meals, we ate well. My parents were therefore surprised when, after a school outing, the teacher told them, much amused himself, about my peculiar culinary taste: I had been so delighted when he had served us soup made from cheap bullion cubes that I had asked him for the recipe and had told him that I had never tasted such wonderful soup at home! Whenever I fussed over food at home, my father would become quite angry and proclaimed that I should live with a farmer's (*Bauer*'s) family to have my fussiness knocked out of me. (A *Bauer* is a low class farmer for which there is no equivalent in the English language.) Strangely, I persisted in refusing to eat what I didn't like!

There are a few things I cannot blame my parents for, unless, of course, I inherited some defective genes. One is a slight red-green color blindness that makes it difficult for me to fully appreciate the Fall colors in New England, but is not severe enough for me to be unable to distinguish between a red or green traffic light. Another deficiency is that I find it difficult to recognize faces. I understand that many people have this defect, which is called prosopagnosia, to a greater or lesser extent, but like color blindness, may not even know they have it. I have a fairly severe case of it. It's socially embarrassing when I don't recognize people, even some of my neighbors, and movies with more than two or three actors usually leave me confused.

My first trusty friend was a large teddy bear that my mother had won at the yearly Dom, a huge fair that is still a yearly event in Hamburg. I loved him dearly. Later, I had a pet, an amiable green leaf frog who lived in a large jar equipped with a ladder and platform on which he could rest. I supplied him daily with mealworms and occasional live flies that my mother had taught me to catch. I can still do that. One has to approach the resting fly cautiously from behind and then quickly scoop it up, being careful not to squash it. It was a sad day for me when the frog died, and later, almost as sad as when my canary, Hansi, gave up his ghost. I dug a small grave for him.

I have never learned to dance well nor to enjoy it. I regret this very much; I often wish I were a Fred Astaire. It's partly because I am self-conscious and afraid to step on my partner's feet, partly because I have trouble detecting the beat of the music. I first became aware of this deficiency in elementary school. Once a year, parents came to watch their children perform. For one of these occasions our class presented an Indian (or was it African?) round dance. We swiped the music from Weil's Threepenny Opera, but cooked up our own lyrics. It was fun. The beat of the music was anything but subtle, but, nevertheless, I was so out of step with the rest of my class that it caused great hilarity among the spectators. Unfortunately I cannot carry a tune either. To this day, I hesitate to chime in during a round of "Happy Birthday To You."

Talking about music brings to mind the first time I helped organize a strike. In our coed music class, the teacher had asked us to sing what we boys disapprovingly considered sappy songs with schmaltzy lyrics about everlasting or unrequited love. Our strike, well planned among us boys, consisted of swearing to silence the next time the teacher was to raise his baton to Schumann's (or was it Schubert's?) *"Du bist wie eine Rose."* I'm afraid the teacher didn't even notice our rebellion; he probably thought that those of us who didn't sing had colds.

My Early Intellectual Interests

One day, a teacher decided to give us what is now called a "thematic perception test." He projected a picture on a screen and asked us to write down what we thought was going on in the scene, just based on the picture. The picture happened to be next to a completely unrelated text and showed a family arguing around a kitchen table. Disregarding the instructions, in vain I tried to relate the picture to the text and made a complete mess of my assignment. The teacher must have doubted my sanity.

Biology was fun – watching tadpoles turn into frogs, for instance. One biology experiment didn't work as well as I had hoped. We had been asked to obtain fertilized hen's eggs – how to tell if they were fertilized, I don't remember – and to incubate them at home at "a warmish temperature." Full of faith, I put half a dozen eggs on our radiator. When the time came for hatching, I eagerly listened for the anticipated cheeps of the chicks. But there were no cheeps, only a nasty smell when I finally broke the eggs.

From early childhood on, I liked doing things with my hands. When I was about twelve, I tried to make a small, working submarine. I got a wooden log, about three feet long, which I sawed in half longitudinally. I then hollowed out each half with a curved chisel. This must have taken weeks. I installed a small battery-driven electric motor attached to a shaft into this cavity. The shaft went through a hole in the rear of the log to a propeller. Finally, I joined the two halves together. Like many great ideas, the project foundered on a slight technicality – I was unable to make a frictionless, yet watertight, seal for the drive shaft. The submarine was never launched.

Another, even grander, project presented itself to me: I would build a perpetual motion machine! (Is there anyone who hasn't thought of it?) The idea was simple: I had a bicycle whose front wheel could be made to drive a small generator that supplied electricity to the headlight. Why not, instead, connect the generator to a small motor? The motor would then turn the wheel, and so, ad infinitum. But, of course, it didn't work. Here, too, friction was my nemesis.

I was more successful in building a headphone radio from a kit. At the heart of this kit was a galena crystal, a forerunner of the transistor that was not invented until about 20 years later. The crystal had to be probed by a fine needle that required frequent readjustment to get optimum reception. Building the kit and listening with earphones to a barely audible local radio station gave me many hours of pleasure. I got even more pleasure from a model electric railroad whose rails took up a large part of my room. Directing the trains around different routes around the track made me feel like the master of my small universe.

I was interested in anything pertaining to electricity. I rugged up a low voltage lamp over my bed so that I could read when I was supposed to sleep, and a switch over the door that shut the light off if my parents came into my room. I suppose my parents knew of the alarm system, but I had fun rigging it up. My dabbling with electricity also led me to impress one of my teachers. The schools gave an oral test to ten-year olds when they had finished grammar school, to determine if the student was to go on to high school or to continue at a trade school. During the test we were asked what electricity was. There was a moment of silence. Then, I stood up and said,

"Electricity is an invisible force that can be used to provide light and to drive machinery." The teacher later called my parents to compliment them on their sophisticated youngster. I easily passed the test (the passport, so to speak) to high school.

My father, who wouldn't have known what a monkey wrench was, much less how to how use one, referred to my do-it-yourself activities as "*basteln.*" This is a hard word to translate, that could mean "handywork" but could also mean "putter." The word implied a slightly contemptuous view of my labors, a put-down that I naturally resented.

When I was about ten years old, I also became interested in the history of science. This came about because the one-pound packages of margarine we bought, "*Echte Wagner*," came with a series of cards that I collected and pasted in an album. A typical card showed picture of a famous scientist or inventor, say Thomas Edison, Louis Pasteur, or Madam Curie, and described their achievements. These inventors and discoverers became my role models, as did Henry Ford whose book, *Das Grosse Heute, das Groessere Morgen*, I devoured. For some reason that I don't remember, one of the "*Echte Wagner*" cards showed swarthy men, wearing sombreros, looking through a picket fence at some hard-working farmers. The picture caption, in Spanish, said, "Que bonito es el trabajo visto des lejos" ("How beautiful is work looked at from a distance"), a saying that I never had occasion to use. How strange that I have remembered it all these years!

Because my parents both worked, I read quite a bit at home. First I remember reading fairy tales and other children's' books, then scary, probably trashy, detective stories by John Kling, and finally, in my teens, a series of juvenile novels by Karl Mai. I don't think there is a boy in Germany who hasn't read Mai. The hero in many of them is a German adventurer who goes to America and travels in Indian territory. He starts as a greenhorn, but soon learns to outshoot, outride, and outdo just about all the white folks he encounters. He eventually makes friends with Winnetou, the chief of the Sioux, whose life he saves. Great stuff, even though Mai himself never came to the States.

Sex Education

My sex education began when I had just emerged from being a toddler and my mother told me that babies were delivered by the stork. According to her, the stork, attracted by a piece of sugar, deposited babies in the chimney from where they descended into the living room. Somewhat later, she added that the stork only visited families where the mother and father loved each other very much. She said this with a sanctimonious voice that I still remember with distaste. I was about five when my mother changed her story. Now babies came from the mother's belly. Though this at least tallied with what I saw around me, it had an unplanned consequence. Shortly thereafter, when we were riding on a crowded streetcar, I asked her if I had been very bloody when I came out of her belly. When she pretended that she had not heard me, I shouted this question again at the top of my lungs. It was not until I was in my early teens and in a Zionist youth group that this information got updated. A leader of the group decided to tell me and the other boys about sex, having first obtained the consent of our parents.

However, I must have been very young when I went swimming and first noticed certain anatomical differences between naked boys and girls, namely, that the girls lacked something that the boys had. I thought that this was interesting but lost no sleep over the discovery. Much later, perhaps at age ten, I also noticed that older girls, closer to my age, had a decidedly feminine wiggle when they walked. Not having studied their anatomy, I decided this was a silly affectation, an ostentatious signal that said, "We are different from you." Had I known of the musical My Fair Lady, I would have sympathized with the song "Why can't a woman be like a man?" It never occurred to me that these observations had anything to do with sex.

It was in an English class when I first saw the word "sex" in print and looked it up in a dictionary. The word struck me as vaguely disturbing, hinting at a secret world that had been hidden from me. This sense of unease was amplified by a story I found in one of my parents' novels. There, a boy and a girl grappled with each other on a lawn, feeling an emotion that was new and strong. I sensed that this was the *geheimniss* (secret) that adults had kept from me.

In the seventh grade, I witnessed a budding romance between a girl and a boy in my class. They were both tall, blond, and very good looking. Her name was Lisaweta Oelkers and I am amazed that I still remember it sixty years later. Lisaweta, probably a Russian name, still sounds mysterious and beautiful to me. Romances between pre-teens in those days were rare, and public handholding, not to mention kissing, was almost unheard of. I don't remember ever speaking to Lisawewta, and I was not jealous of Lisaweta or her boyfriend per se. I did, however, feel that these two had something special that I lacked, and I envied that unnamed, missing something.

My interest in girls was more indirect. I was attracted to a Jewish girl in my neighborhood and often followed her at a distance when she took walks with her sister. In time, I even befriended her and we bicycled together in the suburbs where we lived, but our friendship remained strictly platonic. I was a late bloomer.

A few years later I began to have more serious crushes and I began to follow some attractive girls I knew vaguely at a safe distance. I became a juvenile stalker! Added to this perversity was a bit of a fetish: I thought that girls wearing knee-length boots looked alluring. In those days, most pre-teen kids didn't know much, if anything, about sex and I, certainly, was too naive to know that the allure and sex were related. Today, any six-year-old would set me straight.

Jewish in Germany

Earlier, I wrote about my Jewish ancestors. I will now try to describe how being Jewish affected me and my parents after Hitler came to power. In musical terms, being Jewish was a persistent theme, sometimes joyous, often sad, that accompanied and sometimes directed our lives.

I don't know whether my grandparents had been Orthodox, but for my parents, as later for myself, being Jewish meant having a particular cultural identity, not any specific religious belief. My parents knew no Hebrew, nor were they regular members of a temple or synagogue. On High Holidays, however, they went to a modern temple at the Oberstrasse[15] to show their solidarity with the Jewish people. On Yom Kippur, I took great pride in fasting, but of course never thought more about food than on this holiest day of the year. The services bored me except for the sermons. The Rabbi was a good story teller, like all clergymen worth their salt. He usually took a short passage from the Old Testament and then told us what the passage really meant and what the moral was, and how and why we should take it to heart.

I liked going to Passover dinners at the homes of observant friends. My enjoyment, however, came more from the food, such as matzo dumplings, than from the recitations which were often in Hebrew, which I did not understand. When I was the youngest person present, I had the duty or (or was it a privilege?) to say the "*Ma nishtana halaya hazeh,*" or "Why is this night from all other nights?" The answer was that it was the night, thousands of years ago, that the Jews escaped from slavery in Egypt. During this celebration one chair was always left vacant for the Messiah.[16]

When I was small, we also celebrated Christmas, or at least the pagan side of it. We decorated a tree, lit the candles on the evening of the 24th, sang "*Oh Tannenbaum, oh Tannenbaum wie gruen sind deine*

Blaetter," and exchanged presents. I still think that celebrating Christmas in the evening with the candles providing the only light is more festive than celebrating it in the morning. I liked Christmas with its mystique of candlelight and the smell of pine even better than Passover. I went to bed on those nights full of dreams of all the wonderful toys that would be waiting for me in the morning.[17]

When I was about twelve years old, I went to the Oberstrasse Temple once a week after school and learned a few Bible stories and the Hebrew alphabet. A year later, a rabbi prepared me for my Bar Mitzvah. When the big day came, we went to Oberstrasse Temple and I recited, in Hebrew, in the traditional cantillation, a passage from the Old Testament. For a few minutes I became an actor on a stage. At the time, it felt like an important event, but it had no lasting influence on my life. I am still an agnostic; if there is a God, I hope he will forgive me.

Most of my parents' closest friends were other middle-class German Jews. Many of their ancestors had lived in Germany for centuries and thought of themselves as solid German citizens. Some had served in the German army during WW I. They took pride in famous Jews such as Einstein but showed great prejudice toward newly arrived Eastern European Jews, and tried to emphasize their differences from them. My parents used to scold me for using words like "*chutzpah*" or using my hands to emphasize a point. They would have thought they were looked upon unfavorably by Eastern European Jews because the latter wore sideburns and spoke Yiddish. Though they would have denied it, and may not even have been conscious of it, I think their prejudice was caused by fear that the Gentiles would look with disfavor on the Eastern Jews and fail to distinguish between them and assimilated Jews like themselves. That the Nazis eventually made no such a distinction was a shattering experience for my parents and their friends.[18]

I believe that our apparent blindness to the mortal threat posed by the Nazis, came from the fact that, at least until 1938, the threat came mostly from an anti-Semitic government that, at least in Hamburg, was not especially popular. I was never aware of overt anti-Semitism by the people of Hamburg. Both my parents and I had gentile friends and acquaintances. Among the latter was Rosa, the Catholic woman who had been our cook in the 1920s, and twenty years later helped to save their lives. I will come back to that later. There were also about twenty employees in my father's factory who joined us on a yearly family outing. In 1945, my parents sent food packages to some of them, from Milwaukee, when items like coffee were very scarce in Germany. Later, my parents not only accepted, but loved my Gentile wife. Even during the Nazi years, my parents never complained about the German people as such; their anger and dismay were directed only at the government.

After four years of grammar school and passing the test previously referred to, I went to the Lichtwark School, a twenty minute bike ride from my home. It was a so-called Oberrealschule, similar in some respects to an American high school, and different from the Gymnasium where the emphasis was on Latin and Greek rather than on the sciences. However, it differed from an American high school in that the curriculum was fixed and that the students stayed together in one classroom year after year and that it was the teachers who had to go from one class to another at the end of each hour. Another difference was that we all wore caps with colored bands indicating what year we were in.

I was hardly conscious of being Jewish until about 1933, when I was twelve years old. Hitler had just come into power. My parents were worried about his anti-Semitism, but I was, at first, too young or too naive to be worried. Within a few years Hitler's influence became more pervasive. A year or two after Hitler took over, all Jewish students were ordered by the German authorities to leave the public schools and enroll in Jewish schools. Several teachers expressed their regret to my parents and voiced their strong disapproval of the new laws mandating this separation. I took the transfer to the public Jewish Talmud Tora School in stride. The curriculum and teaching style were similar to what I was used to. Our classes included German, mathematics, history, physics, chemistry, French, and English. Surprisingly, the school was still under the same Nazi-supervised jurisdiction as the other public schools. While most of my new teachers were Jewish, we also had Herr Niemayer, a gentile who taught German. I didn't sense it then, but, in retrospect, I admire him for his courage. Teaching in a Jewish school must have been dangerous for Gentiles.

The main difference between the Talmud Tora School and the Lichtwark School was that, at the Talmud Tora, we had to take classes in religion. There, we read and discussed parts of the Talmud, a compilation of Jewish law. What I liked best was the discussion of legal questions in the Talmud and how the rabbis had adjudicated cases in their role as judges. How, for instance, should a man be fined if his goat had damaged a neighbor's garden? Legal questions still fascinate me.

During my high school years, I wanted to be known as a regular fellow, whatever that meant, but was also attracted to what today we would call nerds. My best friend, Horst Adler, who was nicknamed Tippel, was a regular fellow with whom I played and went bicycling. My parents did not like my having him as a friend because they said that I couldn't learn from him. They seemed to forget that one does not ordinarily choose one's friends to further one's education. Tippel eventually emigrated to France, joined the Resistance movement there, and was killed in action. My nerdy friend was Gerhart Schachney. Schachney was the brightest kid in my class. I sometimes visited him at his home, and enjoyed his company. But I wouldn't call him a chum.

One of our teachers, an Orthodox Jew, sometimes invited me to his house on Friday nights. His family, dressed for the Sabbath, would assemble in their dining room, light the candles and say prayers to welcome the beginning of the holy day. That made a greater impression on me than the holiday services in the temple. I loved these evenings and even now envy those who observe the Jewish Sabbath.

I was never good at sports and felt humiliated when I was usually among the last to be chosen to join a team to play ball at school. In spite of this, I joined a Jewish sports club. I played field hockey, a game that often became quite fierce, and was decidedly unpleasant if you were hit by the stick or puck. What I enjoyed more was rowing in a team on the river Alster that flowed through Hamburg, much as you see on the Charles River. On weekends, we often extended these trips to the much larger river Elbe that flows into the North Sea. We occasionally raced against other teams. One of my greatest pleasures was to be the coxswain, feeling powerful when the boat surged forward at my command.

I probably spent more time on my bicycle than on foot. Often I bicycled to school on Hamburg's many bicycle paths. After school, my friends and I played "chicken" on our bicycles on the quiet Andreasbrunnen Street near my home. The point of the game was to force the other bicyclist to the curbstone. It was a great outlet for aggression. Once, we even spent a few days biking to Brenen, where we stayed overnight. Most of our bikes had only one speed, but we loved them, much as some car-owners cherish their cars, and even decorated them.

At age 10 or so, I went on a camping trip with my friend Harold (Harald) Hamburger and my father in the Lueneberger Heide. I remember only hiking for many miles across the heather, and cooking outdoors on a camping fire. It was a new experience for me. Harold's father was Jewish and had been wounded in WWI with shrapnel that remained in his body. Pieces of it sometimes punctured his skin. I think he had married a gentile and was divorced. Eventually he emigrated to Holland and survived the war. What is so memorable to me is that during WWII, Harold was alienated from his father and joined the German Army. A few years ago, about 2000, I heard from Harold, now a faithful Christian living in South Africa, that he and his father had reconciled.[19]

A few years later, Harold and I spent our summer vacation in a Quaker sponsored camp in Holland near the Zuider Zee. The camp occupied an old castle surrounded by a moat. (In the 1950s, I stopped there to chat with the then-owner. But all I remember is him talking about his marital problems and desire to come to the US.)

At age 14-15 I spent my summer vacation in Denmark because Germany was no longer hospitable to Jews. The first time, a friend and I stayed at the home of a state forester. I remember the kerosene lamps and drinking a special beer with a low alcohol content. The second time, we were more adventurous. We started bicycling, but near the Danish border we checked our bikes and began to hitchhike. It was pretty easy. Whenever we were picked up we made it plain were not Nazis by saying *"Jey . . . Hitler."* (That is, "We don't love Hitler.")[20]

The official anti-Semitism found an outlet in the scandal sheet called "Der Stuermer." It was published by Julius Streicher, Gauleiter of Franconia. The Stuermer was displayed in glass-protected display cases, one of which stood near my home. It contained caricatures of Jewish capitalists and stories of their mythical misdeeds such as ritual murder and rape of Aryan women. It may seem perverse, but I was one of the very few readers who avidly perused its pages. Perhaps my fascination was similar to that of an American seeing himself caricatured by the Soviet press during the Cold War.

The greater Hitler's influence became, the more I became conscious of being Jewish. I joined a secular Zionist youth group called the Habonim, or "The Builders." (There were other Jewish youth groups that were religious.) We talked about emigration long before many of our parents did. Our goal was to become settlers on one of Kibbutzim in Israel. On Friday evenings, we met to talk about the life on the Kibbutz where everyone was to work for the common good. We became convinced that, unlike most Jews in the Diaspora, it would be better for us become farmers and workers. We would become the strong, broad base of the social pyramid. A much smaller part of the pyramid would consist of merchants, and only a very few intellectuals would occupy the top. This was to be in strong contrast to the present, presumably lopsided pyramid where Jewish intellectuals far outweighed Jewish farmers.[21]

I don't want to give the impression that the Habonim offered us only dry lectures on politics and the beauty and duties of a spartan life. We also had fun. We learned to dance the Hora, we sang Israeli songs, we began to get interested in the other sex, and we listened to thrilling stories about how a few of the early Jewish settlers had fought off larger numbers of Arabs. In our eyes, Jewish casualties in Palestine were martyrs for a just cause. It never occurred to us that the Arabs thought that the Jews had misappropriated their land and that they, too, thought they had a worthy cause.

On weekends, we went on outings and overnight trips in the vicinity of Hamburg. Even these prepared us for an expected communal life. We shared food by putting our sandwiches in a pile that was then parceled out. In this way, wealthier kids who brought fancier sandwiches had no advantage over poorer kids who brought plainer ones.

Most of our leaders were still in their teens; I admired them greatly. I copied their dress and parroted their left-wing views which dovetailed nicely with my adolescent rebellion against the bourgeois lives of my parents and their friends. I considered their lives to be soft and unadventurous. Some of our young leaders left Germany even before 1938, because the Nazis threatened them with arrest and deportation to concentration camps.

The War Begins

I graduated from high school with a so-called Einjaehrige certificate in 1938. A few students in my class stayed on for an advanced degree, the Abitur, which would have enabled them to attend university. For middle-class Germans at that time, this was elitist and neither I nor my parents ever considered it.

Instead, I found a job as an apprentice in a small, but well regarded, laboratory that specialized in fuel analysis and was owned by a respected scientist, Dr. Aufhauser. The lab was located in Hamburg's harbor, close to the huge fuel oil storage tanks that lined the river Elbe. Together with my supervisor, Dr. Caro, I often climbed up iron stairways to the top of the tanks to siphon off samples of fuel oil. We then returned them to the lab to test them for their thermal content, that is, the amount of heat produced when a certain amount of fuel oil was burned. We did this by placing a weighed amount of the oil into a heavy-jacketed metal shell, introducing oxygen into this container and immersing it in a known amount of water. We then ignited the oil. The rise in temperature of the water was a measure of the oil's heating value.

Dr. Caro was a 30 year old, Orthodox Jewish chemist. He was always calm and kind. He taught me some laboratory techniques but, more importantly, he taught me, by example, that one could be serious but still optimistic and joyful. I still sometimes think of him. By chance, he and I found ourselves on the same boat that took us from England to the United States in 1940.

That job, however was short-lived because Dr. Aufhauser was also Jewish and his laboratory was closed late in 1938. About the same time my father was pressured, by the Nazis, to sell his clothing factory to non-Jewish owners. We realized that we could not stay in Germany much longer. Because we had no idea how we would make a living abroad, my parents arranged for me to become an apprentice in a welding shop, because they thought that that would be a marketable skill anywhere. During the few weeks I spent there, I learned to electroweld. The difficult thing was to direct the welding rod to the exact spot where I wanted to begin, and then, when I made contact and struck a blinding arc, to immediately cover my eyes with the welding glasses.

Any doubts my parents might have had about leaving Germany were dispelled on November 9, 1938, the day often referred to as Kristallnacht, or the Night of Broken Glass.[22] Officially, it was claimed to be a spontaneous event, a grass roots retaliation for the assassination of a German functionary in the German Embassy in Paris by a young Jew. Actually, the Kristallnacht had been carefully orchestrated by the Nazis even before the assassination. Nazis and their allies beat and even killed many German Jews on that night, and they also destroyed much Jewish property.

On that day, however, since we lived in a suburb far from downtown, we only heard and read that windows of a number of Jewish downtown stores had been smashed. The demonstrations in Hamburg had been relatively mild, since its people had always been more liberal and anti-Hitler than those in other cities. In any case we were not directly affected and thought that the country-wide pogrom was an isolated event.

How mistaken we were! The next day, November 10, by order of the government, all adult male Jews and even half-Jews were rounded up by the local police. The official justification was that they were taken into custody to protect them from the rage of the German people. Instead, after a few days in local police stations, they were sent to concentration camps where millions of Jews died. Since 1933, we had heard whispered rumors of concentration camps but had always assumed these were only for communists and other political dissidents. For this reason, we had always been very careful to keep our anti-Nazi views to ourselves. Now, this precaution no longer protected us.

When my father heard of the roundup he went to the apartment of his sister, my Tante Boebs (Auntie Boebs). When two policemen came to our apartment with orders to arrest him, my mother and I told them that my father was away. They were very polite, even apologetic, but said that they would come back later. I then telephoned my father to tell him what had happened. He decided to come back to us. Later that day, the policemen returned and took him to the local police station. A few days later he and many other Jews from Hamburg were sent to a concentration camp in Sachsenhausen.[23] Had my father not returned from there, I would surely have felt for the rest of my life that my telephone call to him had been the cause of his death.

While my mother tried to find out where he was and petition for his release, I went to various consulates to find ways to leave Germany. Several consulates gave me forms to fill out and told me to put my name on waiting lists. But the Jewish quotas for just about every country were filled. Fortunately, about a month after my father's arrest, the American Consulate in Hamburg issued a visa for my parents to come to the United States. Because of this, my father was released. He never talked about the concentration camp experience; but I will never forget how he looked when we picked him up at the train station, very thin, tired, and dressed in clothes that made him look like a scarecrow.

The lucky arrival of the visa is a story by itself. In the early 1920s, my parents, like many middle class families, had employed a cook. Our cook was named Rosa Hoga. Rosa had some savings in her bank but because of an incipient, skyrocketing inflation was afraid that these savings would be wiped out. My father, as owner of a clothing factory, advised Rosa to invest her money in yarn, which he knew was a commodity that was always needed and that, unlike food, would never spoil. Rosa followed his advice, bought yarn, and sold it again after the inflation had subsided. In this way she did not lose her savings. Around 1925, she emigrated to the United States and worked, again as a cook, for a well-to-do Jewish merchant named Harry Bragarnick, in Milwaukee, Wisconsin. Ten years later she became homesick and returned to Germany. When she returned, she visited my parents in Hamburg. She then opened a little chocolate store in eastern Germany, but returned to visit us in Hamburg about a year later on her way back to her former employer in Milwaukee. She had always been a good Catholic and resented Hitler's opposition to the Church. In 1938, when my parents wrote to her of the worsening conditions in Germany,

Rosa persuaded Mr. Bragarnick, himself a former refugee from Russia, to write an affidavit of support for my family. In the affidavit, he guaranteed that my parents would not become a liability to the United States. It was this document that resulted in the issuance of a visa, the release of my father from the concentration camp, and the eventual emigration of my parents to America.[24]

Though by the end of 1938 we did not anticipate the outbreak of World War II and the death of millions in the German concentration camps, we intensified our efforts to emigrate. This took time. Even after the visas had been issued, permits and passports had to be obtained, belongings sold, and shipping arrangements made. For me and other children a short-cut presented itself when the British government, seeing the worsening conditions of Jews in Germany, opened England's doors to thousands of Jewish children. In this way, I (and perhaps more than a hundred other children under 18) was able to leave Germany by boat in January 1939 on a so-called Kindertransport bound for Southampton. My parents left for the United States a few months later. It was not until 1941 that I joined them there in Milwaukee, Wisconsin, where they had settled near Rosa and the above-mentioned, Mr. Bragarnick.

Chapter 3

Refugee in England

After November 1938, even Jews who had stayed in Germany because they thought themselves German first and Jewish second, began to try to emigrate. The difficulty was not so much to get needed exit permits from the German government, but to get hard-to-obtain entrance visas to other countries. No country freely opened its doors to millions of potential refugees.[25] One of the few exceptions was England, which issued thousands of special visas to German-Jewish children. Provided with such a visa, I said goodbye to my parents in early 1939 and, together with hundreds of other youngsters, boarded a ship in Hamburg that took us to Dover in England. I was quite happy to leave and I did not worry about my parents who had already begun to book passage to the United States; nobody anticipated the Holocaust. More than anything, I looked forward to casting off my childhood and finding adventure in foreign lands.

From Dover, I took a train to London, where I stayed for a few days with the son of a friend of my parents. He was a in his late thirties, a kind man, intelligent, and well-read, perhaps the only intellectual among our family circle. Then I took the train to Birmingham, the home town of the Blankensees who had sponsored me.

For the next six months or so I lived in Edgbaston, an attractive suburb of Birmingham, on Priory Road. The large rooming house was owned by the Blooms. I shared this house with several men about my age, also refugees, and a few native English. Among them was a young English teacher, who was having an affair with one of the older refugees, and an older woman said to be the only female postmistress in Birmingham. We'd eat breakfast – always kippered herring – in the common dining room and then take the streetcar to work. Most English houses in those days did not have central heating. In the evenings, on cold days, we would therefore huddle close the fireplace to chat, in a mix of strongly accented English and German, till teatime at ten, and then go to bed. Our bedrooms were also cold but were provided with metered ceramic gas heaters. In the morning, when we put a sixpence coin into these heaters, they rewarded us with perhaps half an hour of luxurious warmth.

For several months, I worked in a large, multi-storied brick factory owned by the Blankensees' in downtown Birmingham. It made sports trophies. Each trophy was made of two halves that had to be soldered together, a monotonous task at best. The fumes may have been bad for my health.

I had little in common with my co-workers, partly because my high school English had not prepared me for the working class Birmingham accent, an accent often mocked in other parts of England. I began to copy their quaint pronunciation, adding some German gutturals. I suspect that the educated English either smiled or cringed at the way I talked.

There was another problem: I had been brought up to be reasonably polite and was now thrown in with men who equated politeness with effeteness. Their disdain added to my alienation. I was therefore relieved to return to my rooming house in the evening and be in the company of others more like myself.

Fortunately, I met a refugee family from Hamburg, the Pinners. They had left Germany several years ago and had become quite assimilated and prosperous. Their son, Richard, became my friend. The Pinners introduced me to a Dr. Strauss, a chemist, also a refugee, who had brought with him formulae for chemical additives used in foundries. He had started Foundry Services Ltd. and hired me as a lab assistant. In the small laboratory, two other assistants and I did routine chemical analysis of metals. Perhaps if I had been better educated or more mature I would have had more contact with the owner and learned more about chemistry.

I realized my educational deficiencies. I possessed only the so-called 'einjaehriges' high school certificate of graduation from high school and, after work, took in night school classes at Birmingham University to prepare myself for the London matriculation examination. Our professors were always dressed in impressive, traditional black robes. Though passing this examination was a prerequisite for entering any English university, I did not look that far into the future. A university education was beyond my dreams. Even the professors teaching at night were formally dressed in long, black robes.

I lived from hand to mouth, but did not think of myself as deprived. I earned 25 shillings a week, just over a pound, of which 22 and sixpence went for room and board. The few pence it cost to go to a movie were therefore a luxury. I justified this to myself that the movies would be good for me since they would improve my English.

Once, I inquired at a typewriter store about the cost of a typewriter. Later that week a salesman called at my rooming house and showed me a low-cost model for 'only' five pounds. The poor man could not possibly have known that five pounds might as well have been a million. I seem to have heeded Charles Dickens's remark that if one's earnings were one pound and one spent twenty one shillings, that was tragedy; if one spent nineteen shillings – that was bliss.

Yet I lived quite happily within my means. Only once was my financial serenity disturbed: I had accidentally knocked down and broken a vase belonging to my landlady, Mrs. Bloom. To my dismay she demanded 25 shillings in compensation. I thought this was excessive but had to settle by paying her a few shillings a week. There were no movies for me for several months.

Occasionally I rubbed elbows with the well-to-do, the Blankensees', who sometimes invited me to their house or even to outings in their car, or at the Pinner's, who I mentioned above. I enjoyed their hospitality but, in spite of their relative wealth and status I didn't feel inferior to them. One of the Pinner's sons, Richard, wanted to become a conductor. I often watched him as he mock-conducted symphonies while listening to the radio.

During the Spring of 1939, my parents obtained passage from Hamburg to New York with a stopover in England. They visited me for only a day or two and then continued to the United States. It was only a few months later, when World War II had broken out, that we realized what a close call their escape from Germany had been.

That summer I moved to another rooming house in Birmingham with new housemates, also refugees. One was a character actor in his fifties. He worked for a local repertory theater company and spent most of his evenings in front of the fireplace studying his role. When he thought he knew it by heart he would hand the script to one of us nearby to see if he had memorized it correctly.

My roommate was Karl Gold, a few years older than I. He had studied at the University of Vienna and was typically Viennese. By that I mean that he hardly ever took anything too seriously. There is some truth in the saying that a German would describe battle as "serious but not desperate," while a Viennese would call it "desperate but not serious." I owe Karl my interest in good books. He never pushed or lectured to me, but he showed me that not all printed books had equal merit. I loved reading *The Good Earth* by Pearl Buck, a book well suited to my still limited vocabulary. Ever since then I have been an avid reader of literature.

The War Hits Home

On September 1, 1939, Germany invaded Poland. Two days later we listened to the radio as England and France declared war on Germany. But for the next nine months life went on pretty much as usual. It was the calm before the storm, some called it the Sitzkrieg – the "sitting war." The French felt secure behind the Maginot Line – a chain of massive fortifications running the length of their frontier with Germany. The British counted on their large navy for safety. Few people outside Germany expected a large-scale war, and the European democracies only gradually began to put their economies on a war footing.

But the Germans suddenly broke the lull when, in April 1940, they suddenly attacked and conquered Norway and Denmark, and in the next month overran the Netherlands, Belgium, Luxembourg, and France. The British Army, stationed in Europe, retreated to the port of Dunkirk. From there, within one week, they saved 300,000 allied troops by ferrying them to England.

With the fall of France, officially dated with the signing of an armistice on June 21, England now seriously feared an invasion. The army, helped by many tens of thousands of volunteers, took down road signs, or faced them around, to impede the invaders. They even removed signs from railway stations and buildings. They festooned the beaches and cliffs with barbed wire, dug tank traps, set up 'dragon's teeth' and pill boxes, and set up gun emplacements to be fired along the shore as the enemy appeared. In the cities, we had to make our windows light tight to thwart night air raids, and even had to shield our bicycle lamps so that only a dim, narrow strip of light illuminated the pavement.

There was much fear of a Fifth Column. This was an expression derived from the boast of a general in the Spanish Civil War, who said he had four columns outside to besiege Madrid and a fifth column of secret helpers within. Posters captioned "Careless Talk Costs Lives" showed a couple having dinner. One of them said, "Of course, there's no harm in your knowing" – and showed the couple talking at the dinner table, unaware that Hitler was crouching under their table. As a precaution, several hundred of pre-war Fascist sympathizers, including Sir Oswald Mosley, were imprisoned under new Defense Regulations.

Along with about 27,000 other "aliens," I too was interned. Most of us were refugees from Hitler and therefore did not think it was fair to intern us, but we also sympathized with the real danger the country faced. Some internees were later released on condition that they serve in the British armed forces.

I was first sent to Hoyton, near Liverpool, a new apartment complex that had been vacant or vacated for our internment and was now surrounded by barbed wire. The British army was in charge. They treated us as they probably treated their own soldiers – strictly, but fairly. It was not a concentration camp. Like in any army camp, the sergeants often made roll calls to make sure that no one had escaped. They then shouted, "All present and accounted for" to their commanding officer – a phrase that I would often hear repeated in my U.S. Army days. Our quarters and our meals were not luxurious, but adequate. Since milk was scarce, the Quaker-owned Cadbury chocolate factory brought in extra milk for us teenagers. Ever since, I have tried to thank them for their kindness by buying their chocolate. I hope they appreciate that.

I stayed at this camp only a few weeks. Then, a group of us, accompanied by a guard, were sent by train to another camp at the former Lingfield Racetrack, south of London. The horses were gone. Perhaps they had been slaughtered, or been evacuated to places further inland to protect them from German invaders. In the latter case, they were better protected than almost every human being in England. We slept in the now empty stables. Just about every day we had to do some chores, much like years later in the American army. One day, having been ordered by a lieutenant to clean the latrines, I assented with a cheerful "Okydo." That seemed to be the wrong response . . . A burly sergeant – all the sergeants seemed burly – barked at me that I had committed a faux pas and in the future I was to say, "yes, Sir" to an officer, not, "'Okydo." His actual words were less polite.

What I liked best at Lingfield was that some former teachers and professors started a camp university – no fees, no grades – but excellent lectures on a great variety of subjects, such as science and the humanities.

The danger of an invasion was not a paranoid fantasy of the government. This was brought home to us when, beginning in August, we heard the droning of German aircraft passing over our camp at night on their way to bomb British military airports. Though the Luftwaffe lost almost 300 planes in these early raids, it came close to destroying the much smaller British Air Force. This would have been a prerequisite for the invasion that Hitler had planned for September 15.

A fluke saved England. It came about this way: On August 24, German bombers had accidentally dropped some bombs on central London. The next day the British retaliated by bombing Berlin. Now, on September 7, came the turning point of the aerial battle: Furious over the bombing of the German Capital, the Luftwaffe switched their targets from airfields to London. In so doing, they caused tremendous damage to the city, but on that day alone, British fighter planes and antiaircraft batteries shot down hundreds of their planes. Moreover, by allowing the British Air Force bases to repair, regroup, and recover in the weeks to come, the Luftwaffe's targeting London was one of Germany's greatest mistakes in the war.[26]

From the time of their arrival in the United States in 1939, my parents had tried to obtain an emigration visa for me so that I could join them. As a result, just at the time the air raids on London began, I received a letter that my visa was waiting for me at the American Embassy in London. Released from the Lingfield camp, I took a train to London to obtain a passport and to book passage to the U.S.

Life in England had drastically changed during my internment. I found lodging in a rooming house on the Northwest side of London, near Hampstead Heath. Hampstead Heath is a large recreational area on the Northwest outskirts of the city, many miles from its center. During the Middle Ages, Londoners fled there to escape the plague; then it became infamous for its highwaymen. Now, in 1940, large, high-flying balloons, tethered to cables, were anchored there to keep the Luftwaffe from dive-bomber attacks. Large search lights and anti-aircraft batteries dotted the park. Underground, the city had built cement air-raid shelters furnished with cots and latrines.

I never slept in my rooming house because each evening at dusk, the air raid sirens wailed, warning us to seek protection in the underground shelters less than half a mile away. Men, women, and children, rich and poor alike, crowded into these rather safe but bleak cement bunkers. When we got there, there was nothing to do but to lie down on the hard cots. The electric lights were too dim to read by. I thought longingly of the cozy, quiet, safe stables in which I had slept only a week before. Finally, I dozed off amid the comforting boom of nearby anti-aircraft guns.

In the mornings, after the sirens sounded the "all clear" we returned to our rooming house for breakfast. On the way, we saw lots of jagged pieces of anti-aircraft shrapnel on the ground, and less often, bomb craters or destroyed buildings. More than 7,000 tons of bombs were dropped on London during October. Both sides lost hundreds of planes. By the end of the month, 13,000 civilians had been killed and nearly 20,000 seriously wounded in these night attacks. But Hitler was wrong when he had thought his raids would destroy the morale of the people. On the contrary, they seemed less inclined than ever to give up. Churchill spoke of "blood, sweat, and tears" and finished with "We will never surrender." His speech was remembered.

During the day, with fewer air raids, most people carried on with their lives as best as they could. Life during the Blitz was difficult but, to those of us not hurt by the bombs, bearable. Food was rationed. I learned to drink my tea unsweetened and to use a soup extract called Bovril as a spread for my bread. We were scared when the air raid sirens wailed during the day when we were not in shelters and heard the terrifying whine of descending bombs, and a few seconds later, the thunder of explosions. On those occasions one did not think of the death and destruction the bomb had caused, but felt relief that, once again, one's life had been spared.

After waiting for several weeks, I was able to book a passage to Boston on a ship scheduled to sail from Liverpool at the end of January 1941. My last night there, air raid sirens wailed. I felt no need to check into a hotel and slept in a shelter. When the ship raised anchor at dawn the next morning, the docks were aflame; the last I saw were huge black clouds hung over the burning oil tanks in the harbor.

Once again I was a refugee. For twenty years, I did not see England again.

My ship was one of dozens in a convoy. In addition, like caring nannies, several destroyers sailed close by to protect us from German submarines. But how effective was this protection? One day, about halfway between England and America, anxious passengers shouted that they had spotted a submarine in the distance. I rushed forward. Indeed, even without binoculars I could see the outline of a long, grey, monstrous shape surfacing from the ocean depths. A periscope seemed to be rising into the air. Why did the destroyers not fire? Where were the torpedos? The answer was comforting, even if it made us feel sheepish: What we had seen was a whale spouting a column of water.

To my surprise and joy one of the passengers was Dr. Caro, the man I had worked for in Hamburg. We were all escaping from a depressing war and the 'land of milk and honey' lay before us.

One woman, especially, could hardly wait to come within sight of the Statue of Liberty. She was many months pregnant and wanted her baby to be born within the boundary of the United States. In that way, her child would be a U.S. citizen at birth. We were happy for her when we learned that her baby was born only a few hours before we spotted the outline of the coast of America. Her wish was granted.

Chapter 4

Interim Years in Milwaukee (1940-1943)

I arrived in Boston in November 16, 1940[27] and right away hopped on a bus to New York City. The only people I knew there were friends of my parents who lived in upper Manhattan. Needing exercise after the long voyage and unfamiliar with the New York transportation system, I dragged my suitcase many miles, from the bus station in lower Manhattan to their apartment. There I stayed overnight. What most surprised me were not the skyscrapers for which I was prepared, but the great heft of the Sunday newspapers compared to the skinny ones in Europe.

The next day, I took the train to Milwaukee, Wisconsin. As the train entered the city, I was disappointed to see a multitude of shacks and rickety wooden houses along the railway track. I had expected everybody in America, the richest country in the world, to live in splendid houses made of stone, the material used for European mansions. I realized only later that many exquisite American houses were crafted from wood.

My parents had arrived in Wisconsin in 1939 more or less penniless. For a few months, they were servants for a well-to-do family on a large estate near Milwaukee. When I joined them in 1941, they lived in an apartment in North Milwaukee. Later, we moved to a large flat on the second floor of a house at 2905 North Marietta Ave. It was a great location, just a block from Lake Park on Lake Michigan.

The flat was in a house still heated with coal, the most common fuel of the times. When we felt chilly, and sweaters would not longer do, either my father or I went down a narrow, rickety stairway into the dimly lit basement and groped for the huge, black, now almost cold furnace in the far corner. We opened the furnace door and were greeted by a small, but promising, pile of glowing embers. First, we scooped out the ashes from under the grate and ladled them into buckets. Then, we dug into the coal bin and heaped its black nuggets, shovel by shovel, into the furnace's belly. Now the waiting began. We stared into the furnace. Had we added too much coal and smothered the embers? Nothing happened, nothing at all. We picked up a cast iron poker and stoked the coal. More anxious waiting. Then, suddenly we saw a tentative flicker, then another; tiny licks of flames, but flames they were. Our anxiety turned into jubilation. The flames quickly spread from coal to coal. The furnace became a small inferno of dancing, crackling yellows that made our faces glow. A great sight. For several minutes we enjoyed the show. Then, our task done, we trudged upstairs, almost reluctantly, but assured that in an hour or two, our flat would again be cozy.

To help pay the rent, my parents had taken in two borders, Dr. Bamburger, with whom I shared a room, and Dr. Bardach. In Vienna they had been lawyers, but now Dr. Bamberger peddled Fuller brushes and Dr. Bardach worked as a clerk. They were excellent story raconteurs. I suspect that they knew more intimate details of European royalty than they knew of their own estranged wives and children. Since for me, history had stopped in high school with Napoleon, I now realized what an utter ignoramus I still was. Dr. Bamburger later became a close friend of my aunt Miez, who came to live with my parents for a few years after the war. Even later, he joined her when she moved to New York City. During his last years there he taught Latin at the Rudolf Steiner School. Dr. Bardach died of cancer during the war while I was away.

My father became a traveling salesman. He first sold lingerie to families who wanted to help a new immigrant. Later, after he had bought a car and learned to drive, he became a representative for New York-based manufacturers and travelled across Wisconsin calling on jewelry stores. My mother often earned money by knitting gloves and the like for an acquaintance who had begun to manufacture such items. To their credit, my parents never complained that they were much poorer than they had been in Germany. They were well aware how lucky they were to have escaped.

I was in my late teens, had tasted independence, but was now again a child in my parents' home. Once more, I felt like an alien. Instead of being overjoyed at having escaped from Nazi persecution and from war-torn

England to a country at peace, I was at first appalled at finding Americans oblivious to the war in Europe.

Shortly after I arrived from England, I had a chance to go to college. A Jewish fraternity at the University of Wisconsin invited me to visit them in Madison and then offered me a scholarship. But my parents urged me not to accept it because my father's earnings were small and my contributions were needed. In retrospect, my decision not to accept the scholarship seems shortsighted; at the time it made sense to me. I was still rooted in the world of my parents and I did not even think of an academic or professional career. I declined the offer.

I had no close friends – only acquaintances. I was lonely, but often too busy to be aware of it. My parents played bridge several times a week and had more of a social life. Occasionally, we visited Rosa Hoga, who now lived in a Catholic old age home, and Mr. Bragarnick, her former employer, who had made it possible for my parents to come to the United States. Both of them were then in their 60's and ailing. Among my parents' other acquaintances were two elderly sisters, former teachers, both unmarried, and quite featureless; they were the most boring, unfailingly insipid people I have ever met. But they were kind, and I felt guilty in disliking them. Perhaps this is why I still remember them.

I tried various jobs. One of them was to demonstrate Hoover vacuum cleaners in a department store repeating the slogan, "It cleans, while it beats, while it sweeps" to dismayingly disinterested shoppers. Whatever talents a demonstrator needed, it quickly became evident that I did not have them.

I also tried to become a taxicab driver. First I learned to drive. Then, clutching my drivers license, I applied for a job as taxi driver. There was a hitch, however: First, together with other applicants, I had to take a written test that required knowledge of Milwaukee's roads. Only a native could have answered questions, such as "How would you drive from East Podunk Ave. to North Hamilton Road?" Since, as far as I was concerned, these streets might as well have been on the moon, I feigned a headache, and slunk out of the classroom taking the test home. A week later I took the same test again, and crime sometimes pays, did very well. But I never became a taxicab driver. A more appealing job came along.

The new job was to sell magazines from house to house in lower middle class areas. I would ring the doorbell and begin my sales pitch, to the lady of the house. The pitch was to obtain a one-year contract for weekly deliveries of three magazines. There were dozens to choose from and the weekly cost was small. To sweeten the deal, the subscriber got a free set of collected works by popular authors. If asked how so much could be obtained for for so little, I would explain - and I think this was true - that most of the cost was borne by the magazine advertisers. What I did not care to spell out was that even a few pennies a week would add up to many dollars in a year.

With having hardly anyone outside my family to chat with, I rather liked this job. The housewives, too, seemed to like the interruption from their daily tasks. So often, they asked me to come back in the evening when their husbands were home, that I began to work only in the evenings. I took it easy during the day and often went swimming in Lake Michigan. Since few households had television sets, and people depended more on magazines for entertainment than they do now, I made an easy living during my first summer in the America.

Perhaps it was the prospect of better pay that made me take on the worst job I ever had. It was in a factory in West Milwaukee about an hour's streetcar ride from my home. The factory made welding rods, coated iron bars, rapidly spat out by a machine onto a conveyor belt. The belt then carried them through a high temperature tunnel for baking. My job was to sit between the machine and the tunnel and to separate the bars so they would not stick together. This went on for eight hours with only a thirty minute, short break for lunch. If I had to relieve myself, I had to raise my hand for a stand-in. During my first days, the constant motion of the moving bars made me sick in my stomach. I got used to the motion, but never to the monotony. My only relief came when, occasionally, the machine ran out of coating material or had a mechanical problem. Those were moments to rejoice. The factory worked three shifts. I liked the night shift best since it allowed me to enjoy at least a few hours of daylight.

Happily, this job only lasted a few months. Because of my work in England, I found a better job as lab assistant at the huge Harnischfeger Corporation, manufacturer of earthmoving equipment. I shared the small lab with two other assistants, supervised by Mr. M.T. Morris. Unless something went wrong, we hardly saw him. Our task was to test the physical and chemical composition of the steel that went into the company's products, to ensure that the steel met their standards. In one test, we first turned the steel into bars, then pulled them in a tensile tester until they elongated and finally burst. In another test, we polished a small sample of the steel, etched it, and examined its structure through a microscope. For a third test, we pressed a hardened steel ball into the test specimen; the diameter of the resulting indentation then gave us a measure of its hardness.

We also tested for carbon, and alloying metals. Often, time was of the essence. Then, I had to dash to the foundry, scoop up a sample of molten, fuming, red-hot steel from a huge cauldron, and rush it to the laboratory to be analyzed. If we found a deficiency, or excess of carbon or manganese, we would call the foundry right away, so they could make needed correction before pouring the steel into molds.

One bright side of these (not so satisfactory) interim years was that I began to educate myself (stumbingly, haphazardly, and without guidance), into the world of books and ideas. The love of books and ideas has stayed with me all my life and grown through the years. I love the saying attributed to Logan Pearsall Smith: "People say that life is the thing, but I prefer reading." Even when I take my daily bath, I place a book within reach. I may never read it, but it's nice to know it is there. Children have their security blankets; mine are books.

I fondly remember reading the essays by Lewis Mumford who opened my eyes to technology gone wild. I started to read "The Nation" with its critique of American politics, but I was upset to find this country not as perfect as I had imagined and wanted it to be. I read John Steinbeck, Jane Austen, Willa Cather, and J.P. Marquand's "The Late George Apley," a delicious satire of Boston society, so subtle that I did not then catch its satiric intent. At the time of writing this (Spring, 1995) I remembered this book and chose it as one of the texts for a course on satire that I am giving at the Harvard Institute of Retirement.

Milwaukee is a city of close to a million, dating back to an Indian settlement in the 17th century. In the middle of the 19th century, it grew rapidly as a result of political refugees from Germany who founded the city's famous beer industry. My parents and I and most of our friends belonged to a later influx of refugees from Nazi Germany. Milwaukee was clean, had beautiful parks along Lake Michigan, several colleges, and a great zoo. But I was not happy there, and remember Milwaukee largely as a large, gray, sprawling, and somewhat boring, provincial town without much glory.

The war I had left behind finally caught up with me in December 1941 when the Japanese bombed Pearl Harbor and drew the United States into the war. As had been true in England, lifestyles for most of us were slow to change. I continued to work for the Harnischfeger Corporation, now flush with defense contracts. Then, in March 1943, I received my induction notice from the local draft board to report for service in the Army of the United States.

Chapter 5

You are in the Army Now[28]

In March 1943, I received a postcard from the War Department. "Greetings," it began, "you are hereby ordered for induction into the Army of the United States, and to report at . . ." So began my military service. The U.S. had declared war on Japan on December 8, 1941 after Japan's sneak attack on the U.S fleet at Pearl Harbor. In response, Germany, Japan's Axis ally, had declared war on the United States. Now, more than two years later, the Axis and Allied forces were still engaged in fierce battles in the Pacific, the Atlantic, in North Africa, and in Russia.

I reported to my local draft board in Milwaukee on March 13 and was sworn in as a private, the lowest rank for soldiers. I had seen movies where the departing soldiers smartly marched off to war to the tune of military bands and cheering crowds, but the movie makers had evidently not taken their inspiration from the induction center in Milwaukee. There was no music, and there was no crowd. I haven't looked up the weather report for that day, but in my recollection it drizzled, matching my mood. Several fellow draftees and I were then rounded up and shipped by train to a so-called boot camp near Chicago.

On the way, I wondered what would be in store for me. I was proud and even happy to have become a soldier. I wanted Germany and Japan defeated; and after some dispiriting years in Milwaukee I looked forward to adventure, even saw myself as a possible hero. On the other hand, I had read enough about World War I to know that war can be hell, and that I might come back injured or in a coffin.

At boot camp I was assigned to a barracks and given a uniform, a rifle, a footlocker, a canteen, and dog tags with my name, rank, and serial number to hang around my neck. But it wasn't until I was subjected to a closely clipped G.I. (Government Issued) haircut that I felt I was really in the Army. Now the Army controlled my life. I had lost my freedom and my privacy. If I had been older I might have felt devastated. But I was young and had neither taste nor time for introspection. I adjusted with remarkable ease.

College graduates and professionals had usually obtained deferments or entered the armed forces as commissioned officers. Most of my fellow GIs were under 30 and had, at best, a high school education. To vent their frustrations and to prove their manhood they liked to spike their sentences with obscenities. Those like me who'd been deficient in our use of expletives, quickly added them to our vocabulary. I was then able to join the many long and serious conversations about the fucking Army, the fucking food, and the fucking Army.

Civilians are motivated by promotions, love and praise, but seldom fear. But in the Army, fear comes first. Praise is nearly unknown, and promotions from private to corporal or corporal to sergeant are rare. Most soldiers most of the time are not actively fighting an enemy, so their main motivation is fear of anyone above them in the military hierarchy. The Army depends on that fear to prevent chaos. The soldiers' only chance of keeping their fear at bay is to keep their noses clean by blind obedience to their superiors.

Our immediate fear was to incur the wrath of a non-commissioned officer – a corporal or, worse, a sergeant – for being out of step during a drill, or for having a button missing during our daily inspection. More remote was our fear of a dishonorable discharge from the Army, a life-long blemish. Our worst fear, only whispered or dreamt about, was the fear of a court martial for insubordination or neglect of duty. Soldiers learn to be at least as afraid of their own superiors as of the enemy – perhaps even more so.

Our fear never went away, but it retreated from our consciousness. Only occasionally, such as when we were scolded, did it surface. Every day we were called out for drills where we had to carry out commands – "present arms," "right shoulder arms," "left flank march" and the like, much like circus animals or robots – quickly, precisely, without thinking.

A week or two into boot camp, several soldiers and I were sent to a camp near La Jolla, Southern California, for basic training. Though it was an anti-aircraft establishment, I learned little about shooting down enemy planes. Every day we were woken at dawn by a peppery, unbearably cheerful bugle call to the melody of "You Got to Get Up, You Got to Get Up, You Got to Get Up in the Morning." Then we had to 'fall out' and assemble for roll call to ensure that everyone was accounted for. At the same time the corporals or sergeants also inspected us for infractions, like spots on our uniform. Those who were sick could ask for permission to go the infirmary. Sometimes, to the disgust of everyone, a soldier changed his place and forced a recount. If all went well, the sergeant would then shout to the company lieutenant, "All present and accounted for, Sir!" and we would make a dash for the mess hall for chow.

Our days were spent on exhausting marches and strenuous calisthenics, attending assemblies and lectures on weapons, and learning to disassemble, clean, and reassemble our rifles, even in pitch blackness. Every day ended with the hauntingly mournful tune of taps. At least once a week we had to watch the same mind numbing sex education films. Their message, clumsily told, was that any woman we might meet outside camp was sure to carry venereal disease. The best thing about these screenings was that I could take a refreshing nap as soon as the lights went out. But the Army rightly suspected that the anti-sex films might not suffice to keep us saintly. So, to save us from our carnal instincts, rumor had it the Army added saltpeter to our diet. But it did not fully trust the calming effect of saltpeter either and subjected us to frequent 'short arm' inspections by medical personnel. I wonder how many lifelong misogynists the Army created this way!

All too often we saw our names on a "KP" (kitchen police) list. This meant getting up about 5 a.m. and slaving in the mess hall for eight hours. It seemed like an eternity. One memorable day, I was told to put all the potatoes for the company's dinner into a peeler which looked and worked like a washing machine except that the inside of the barrel was rough. Friction removed the potato skins. I turned the peeler on but, alas, forgot to turn it off in time. The potatoes that emerged were the size of peas. The mess sergeant was not happy with the results, and was in fact close to apoplexy. His swearing surpassed anything I had heard before, both in volume and duration.

The only thing worse than KP was night guard duty. This meant I had to get up at midnight and walk around a block of barracks for four hours, a rifle slung over my shoulder. I had been given the password for the day and was to challenge anyone I encountered. But the area was deserted and the nights seemed endless. Bleary-eyed, I trudged round and round the block for what seemed an eternity. Only the threat of a court martial kept me from sitting down for a rest. At dawn, another soldier came to relieve me from my ordeal. He seemed like one sent from heaven.

We were also had to prepare for anti-aircraft service. The programs consisted of lectures and films teaching us to differentiate between the silhouettes of friendly and enemy planes. I often forgot the subtle distinctions, and shudder to think of the havoc I would have caused – downing Allied planes by 'friendly fire' – if I had become an anti-aircraft gunner.

After a few months in this camp, the new Army Specialized Training Program (ASTP) came to my rescue. The ASTP was meant to keep American colleges and universities from being decimated during the war and to assure an adequate supply of college educated men during and after the war. I scored high enough on an Army intelligence test to be chosen for this college program. I was delighted to suddenly find myself largely free from the military tedium, and transformed, though still in uniform, into a freshman engineering major.

For two semesters (see appendix for college transcript), I was stationed at Pomona College, South of Los Angeles. Suddenly, I found myself on a beautiful campus within sight of the mountains, with fellow students more intelligent than those I'd left behind and with pretty coeds in sight as I began a college education. It was pure heaven.

At the start of the first semester, the Army ordered me report to the Los Angeles District Court to become a naturalized citizen. I had only been in the United States about three years and, normally, would have had to wait another two years before obtaining citizenship. The Army waived the five-year stipulation to keep me from being shot as a traitor had I been captured by the Germans. After listening to a long, quite inspiring speech by the presiding judge about the privilege of becoming an American I, and dozens of other soldiers, was sworn in as a citizen of the United States, on July 2, 1943. I was twenty-one years old.

In December 1943 our class was reassigned to the ASTP engineering program at the University of Oklahoma in Norman. I studied there for one more semester. (See the appendix for college transcript.) By comparison with the orange groves in Pomona, the Norman campus, rimmed by reddish soil dotted with oil rigs, was bleak. But I continued to delight in college life. The courses were more challenging and specialized than those at Pomona. I liked my classes and did well, except in mechanical drawing. I could never see a three dimensional body by looking at two two-dimensional views. It stumped me then, and it still does. Later, as a professional physicist, I always preferred to make mockups-sometimes from cardboard and Scotch

Tape - and let engineers turn these crude models into drawings and, eventually, into respectable hardware.

During this semester one student, John Hunter, accidentally electrocuted himself by touching a high-tension wire in one of our laboratories. His was the only death I knew during all my years in the Army. John had been an experienced radio operator before he had joined the Army and knew much more about electricity than any of us. I have been exceedingly respectful of electricity ever since; the memory of John's accident may have saved the lives of many of his comrades.

At the end of the semester we had a one week furlough. I spent mine with my parents in Milwaukee. When I returned in March, 1944, the Army told us that the ASTP program had been discontinued and that I had been reassigned to the Signal Corps at Camp Crowder in Missouri. This news put a sudden, unexpected end to my dreams of getting a college education while in the Army. At Camp Crowder, I was assigned to a teletype repair school till a test showed, to my surprise, that I was slightly red-green color blind. Since the wires leading into the teletype machines were color-coded, my color blindness would have raised havoc. Instead, I was sent to a Diesel engine maintenance and repair school where, it was hoped, I would do less harm.

The Signal Corps needed Diesel engines to drive the electric generators used in radio and other forms of communication. They were like gasoline engines except that, after the operator started them on gasoline, he closed off a section of the combustion cylinder to increase the compression. He then switched the engine to diesel fuel oil. The engine now continued to run without spark plugs. I attended this school for several weeks and spent another few weeks getting hands-on experience maintaining Diesel engines.

One weekend, to get away from the camp, I hitched a ride to Atlanta. The city was swarming with soldiers. With hundreds of others, I had to find shelter and sleep on the floor of a church. On other weekends, I took flying lessons in a Piper Cub at a local airport. The small planes made it easy to learn. They had dual controls, one for me and one for the instructor, who could override any of my mistakes. Among the things I had to learn was to "bank" the plane, to tilt it just the right amount when turning. I also had to learn the subtle relation between the speed of the plane and its ability to climb. If, for instance, the plane didn't travel fast enough when I pulled the control stick to climb, it would begin to fall like a leaf into an uncontrolled spin. Though this was scary, the instructor often had me do this on purpose so as to learn not to panic. To regain control, I had to push the stick forward

– against my instinct – and, by making the plane dive further, make it pick up speed. Only then could I regain altitude. I had hoped to obtain a student license to fly solo, but I did not stay at Camp Crowder long enough to log the needed flight hours. I never took up flying again.

The Signal Corps demanded we climb 90 ft. high telephone poles to string telephone lines or radio antennas. To climb these poles, we had to strap sharp metal spikes to our boots. Like today's telephone linemen, we wore a leather belts around our waist and around the pole. The belt was loose enough for us to lean away from the pole as we climbed while the spikes on our boots dug into its wood. This went well, except as we neared the top and looked down, one of us got dizzy and instinctively hugged the pole. The spikes then no longer dug into the wood at an angle and the poor climber rapidly slid down, collecting splinters all the way. By the time he hit the ground, he looked like a porcupine. Before I had mustered the courage to climb to the top, I was due for a week's furlough. I went to Milwaukee and put the hated poles out of my mind. (See the essay at the end of this chapter for more detail about the poles.)

This time, good news awaited my return. During the past year I had repeatedly tried to get into Counter Intelligence because, so far, the Army had wasted my knowledge of German. Counter Intelligence also conjured up romantic images of cloak and dagger and high adventure. I had made many long, formal applications for a transfer but nothing had happened. Then, by luck, I obtained the name of an adjutant at Camp Ritchie, a military intelligence training center in Maryland. The adjutant was a woman who'd been able to rise through the male Army hierarchy. I wrote her a short personal 'Dear Madam' letter explaining that my transfer to Camp Ritchie would well serve the Army. Returning from my furlough, I was called into the office of the commandant of Camp Crowder and told that my transfer to Camp Ritchie had been authorized. This experience taught me that it often pays to bypass official channels.

Camp Ritchie lies in the Blue Ridge Mountains in Maryland, some miles from Washington, D.C. The camp trained soldiers to interrogate prisoners of war. This had to be done within the framework of the Geneva Convention which guaranteed a prisoner of war that he need only divulge his name, rank, and serial number. To circumvent this in actual battle conditions without breaking the law, prisoners were usually interrogated at or near the front lines immediately after capture. Timely intelligence about the deployment of enemy troops was then most vital. Furthermore, the prisoners were then often still dazed and yielded to mild forms of deception and coercion. We could, for instance, assure the prisoners that by talking to us they would not in any way betray their comrades, but merely verify what we already knew. Less subtly, we could also point out to them that the Geneva Convention allowed us to imprison them in any Allied prisoner of war camp. That meant that, depending on their cooperation, we were therefore free to send them either to the United States or to Russia. There was no need to ask them which country they preferred.

Since we could not expect prisoners to speak English, the interrogator-trainees had to be bilingual. Most of them, like myself, were German refugees. The training was intensive. Classes were held all for day for several weeks. To become good interrogators we had to learn the composition of the German Army from battalion level down to the last squad, to recognize all of their insignia, and to be familiar with all of their weapons. We became more familiar with the German Army than with our own. We also had to become experts in reading maps. During night maneuvers we were only given maps, compasses, and directions to meet at a specified location. Toward the end of the program we had to conduct mock interrogations. A member of the camp staff played the part of the prisoner. He had a detailed script of their troop disposition. We, in turn, were judged by how much of this information we could extract.

On weekends I often hitched rides to Washington, D.C. where I enjoyed visiting the air-conditioned museums during the hot, humid summer. Once I even went to New York and attended a nationally broadcast show at Radio City. Since I was the only soldier in the large, mostly female audience, the master of ceremonies picked on me to join him on the stage. He asked me my name and where I was stationed. "What kind of camp is that?" he inquired. I could not very well answer "military intelligence" since that was supposed to be a military secret not be broadcast to thousands or even millions of viewers. I hesitated what for me seemed an eternity before telling him that Camp Ritchie was an infantry camp. A lie in this case seemed preferable to facing a possible court martial case.

By the time I graduated in July 1945, Germany had already surrendered, but the war with Japan continued. I regretted that I never got to practice what I had so painstakingly learned at Camp Ritchie, but, as if to compensate, the Army told me they wanted me to become a commissioned officer. This made me very happy, especially since I had only recently arrived in the U.S. as an immigrant refuge. I was 24 years old.

Since Camp Ritchie was not authorized to commission its graduates, I was temporarily assigned for three months of grueling training to the infantry officer candidate school (OCS) at Fort Benning, Georgia. Its mandate was to turn us into infantry officers who could lead men into battle. My class consisted of a company of four platoons, each platoon made up of 20 men under constant, close scrutiny by a tactical officer. Compared to OCS, my former basic training seemed like Kindergarten. I remember two activities, especially. In one, we had to dig foxholes and jump into them just seconds before tanks overran our position. In another, more entertaining and less scary, we learned to get a Jeep across a river without bridges by driving it to the river's edge onto a huge tarpaulins that we wrapped and tied around it. We then pushed the contraption into the water and floated it to the other shore. I have no figures on what it cost to train us, but it must have far exceeded the cost of a first-rate college education.

Near the end of our training, we had to rate one another in confidential ballots – who would make the best officer, who the worst? This so-called 'buddy rating' enabled the officer in charge to compare his own judgment of a man with the opinion of the man's peers. In this way, our ability to judge was itself judged and could lead to our dismissal from OCS. Since we knew from the start of OCS that we would eventually be rated by our comrades, we were also more considerate of them than we might been otherwise.

We lost about third of the men in our platoon before the end of the three months. The Army gave no reason for their dismissal. Those of us who survived, facetiously called "90 day wonders," graduated on September 10, 1945, just a few weeks after the U.S. dropped atomic bombs on Hiroshima and Nagasaki, and a few days after Japan's surrender. We got honorable discharges as enlisted men and instantly reappointed as 2nd lieutenants. As an officer, I had to buy my own uniform but got paid more. I was very proud when I fastened my new brass bars to my lapel. (See the appendix for my graduation brochure with photographs of our class and the text of our oath to "support and defend the Constitution of the United States.")

OCS was the most demanding period in my life. Though I never had a chance to practice what I learned, surviving the rigorous training made me more self-assured. My bar mitzvah, which was supposed to have marked my becoming an adult, had not changed me; OCS did. (Would it be desirable, I wonder, if all young people had to go through some ordeal which they could later look back on with pride, a difficult initiation into adulthood?)

After obtaining my commission, I returned to Counter Intelligence at Camp Ritchie. Since Americans soldiers were no longer needed in Europe, I received orders to go to Japan. I did not know a word of Japanese and was puzzled why I would be sent to the Orient. The Army's decision, however, was not as senseless as I had thought. My fluency in German became very useful. I'm glad that I was given the chance to see Japan and, later, China.

I was flown first to Hawaii. My layover in Honolulu was not long enough to leave the airport. With time to kill, I confidently ambled into to a large well-appointed salon. At the entrance a sign read 'General Officers Lounge.' I took this to mean 'officers of all ranks,' but I soon discovered my assumption was mistaken. I had just begun to snooze in a luxurious chairs when a guard woke me and respectfully but firmly he informed me that only generals were allowed in these sacred quarters. I had trespassed. As a new officer, I still had a lot to learn.

The next stop on our flight was Guadalcanal, part of the Solomon Islands in the Pacific, the site of long and fierce battles. Now, all that was fierce was the heat. Soldiers lolled along the beaches and monkeys chased each other. After a short stay we flew on to the Philippines. This country had also been ravaged by the war and had been liberated quite recently. It was still in a state of chaos. We were quartered for a couple of weeks in a tent city hastily built on the outskirts of Manila. There, too, the heat was daunting. Since I had no duties to speak of, I used some of my spare time to attend the court martial of General Yamashita, the former commander of the Japanese Army of occupation. The American prosecutor charged that Yamashita was responsible for the numerous and terrible atrocities his troops had committed against Filipino civilians. The prosecutor won the case; Yamashita was later executed. I still wonder whether Yamashita should have been held accountable for the behavior of his troops. Would we hold one of our own commanding officers responsible for crimes committed by American soldiers? And if not, what does it say for justice?

We left the Philippines late in 1945 for Japan on the S.S. Kinkaid, an old, converted freighter. I was in charge of a deck-cleaning detail but hardly any men showed up. Most of them were either seasick or drowsy, as I was, with Dramamine. I am afraid that during this voyage the S.S. Kinkaid did not get the thorough scrubbing she deserved.

Early in January we docked in Yokohama where, as in the rest of Japan, food was still scarce. From the deck we saw dozens of hungry, emaciated Japanese dockhands. As I watched the unloading of hundreds of food-containing crates from our ship I had an idea. I asked our crew operating the winches and cranes to '"accidentally" drop a few crates so that they would break and spill their contents. The crew fell in with this with gusto. For once the Japanese dockhands had enough to eat. It is true that our action was illegal. It is true also that it was not we but the American taxpayers who paid for our magnanimity. But at that time I think all of us on board the ship felt we had done the right thing.

Yokohama is only a stone's throw from Tokyo. I was quartered in a large, hotel, almost within sight of the Imperial Palace. I stayed there for only a week and was then assigned to the Gora Hotel about an hour's train ride away and located in scenic hills near Mt. Fuji. It was small but posh and well-staffed by Japanese. Our small Counter Intelligence unit shared the hotel with about half a dozen formerly high-ranking German prisoners. They occupied comfortable rooms which they were not free to leave without being accompanied by a guard. At mealtime they were marched to the dining hall where they remained standing at the table till their ranking member was seated. I thought that this insistence on rank and order was a bit comical and typically German. One day, the Germans sent a formal note to our commanding officer complaining that the meat they had been served was too tough. To my amusement the cook was ordered to grind up that meat and to serve it again the next day as Hamburgers. I understand that the Germans savored their dinner. There were no complaints.

The officer I got to know best was General Kretchmer. At one time, he had been in charge of the supplying the German armed forces for the intended invasion of England. He told me that he had completed this task when, at the last minute, the invasion was called off by Goering. Kretchmer said the German Airforce had experienced such heavy losses over England that it would have been unable to provide adequate air cover for the invading fleet. I talked to him often and helped translate a report he was preparing of his war-time experiences. It's a pity I did not keep a copy.

For recreation, I often I took a jeep to a nearby natural spa. As is the custom in Japan, we first washed and rinsed ourselves in separate tubs. Only when cleansed did we enter naked into the large communal bath that was shared by both sexes. The water, being of volcanic origin was so hot that that we were advised not to stay in it for more than ten minutes. Even after leaving the bath and driving back to our hotel in an open jeep in winter time our bodies were still so warm that we easily tolerated the chilly air.

I stayed at the Gora Hotel for only a month or two. My next assignment was to a large internment camp near Karuizawa. It was located in a lovely mountain valley about an hour's train ride west of Tokyo. The camp had formerly been a popular, vacation resort for foreign nationals. Now, though surrounded by barbed wire, it retained much of its former charm. Most of the German and other foreign nationals in Japan at the time of the surrender had been transferred to this camp.

Here, I met General Kretchmer again. No longer in the military, he spent much of his time studying the writings of the 19th century philosopher-mystic Rudolf Steiner. Kretchmer was an intelligent, serious scholar, a far cry from the heel-clicking stereotype of the German generals as shown in the American movies at that time. His eighteen-year-old daughter, Mickie, became a good friend of mine.

I didn't have much to do, except to interview German families within the compound and report my findings to Headquarters in Tokyo. Many of the Germans denied or downplayed having had any sympathy or connections to the Hitler regime. Some of them even showed me documents that proved that an ancestor of theirs had been Jewish, a fact they had hidden during the Nazi period. They all preferred to stay in Japan where conditions were better than in post-war Germany. I never found out which of the Germans were sent back, but rumor had it that a few that should have been sent back had established friendships with high-ranking American officers who saved them from deportation.

One day in March, 1946, I had to accompany a certain Herr Lissey, to a Bank in Tokyo where he was said to have deposited a large number of diamonds. My assignment was to receive these diamonds and to convey them to the American headquarters. When we opened the safe I had expected to see a sparkling treasure but only found a small bag filled with uncut, unpolished dirty-looking gravel. Because I had no proof that they were really diamonds, I only acknowledged that I had received a certain number of "stones."

In July, with my Army discharge date approaching, another officer and I volunteered to spend a few weeks traveling through Northern Japan as paymasters for half a dozen or so Counter Intelligence Units. This gave us a great opportunity to see the country. We were given big bags containing tens of thousands of Yens, as well as pistols to protect us from being robbed. The weapons were quite useless to us, however, since we had never been taught how to use them. We traveled mostly by train in the special cars reserved for the U.S. military. First we went north along the east coast to Sapporo in Hokkaido, the northern island of Japan, then back along the west coast of the main island back to Tokyo. The trip took about a week.

It was fun and fairly incident free. Once, we were already on a train when we suddenly realized in a panic that we had forgotten our money bags at our CI unit in Sapporo. Each of us had thought the other had brought it along. We hopped on the next train back and, much to our relief, found the bags just where we had left them.

My honorable discharge from the Army on August 7, 1946 was based on length of service. I could have chosen to be discharged in the U.S. but chose instead to receive my discharge in Japan at the Tachikawa airbase near Tokyo. I had begun to like much of Japan, especially the terraced hills in the country, the plaintive music, the simplicity and the airiness of the houses. My main regret was, and still is, that Army regulations had forbidden us to fraternize with the people. My contact with the Japanese was therefore mostly limited to waiters and tradesmen. Even today I do not know if the friendliness we experienced was genuine. I also had other reasons for wanting to stay for at least another year. I had made friends with several Americans and civil service jobs were readily available.

World War II made me neither a hero nor a coward. I never experienced a battle except to participate in simulated maneuvers. I was never sent overseas till after the Japanese had capitulated. I never saw blood or dead bodies. But, though I had never experienced the grimness of war, my three years in the Army had changed me. I had gone in as a half-baked youth and I came out as a young man – if not much wiser, at least more self-assured.

SPECIAL SECTION: *The Army and I*

Helmut's Essay about the Dreaded Pole, the Army Experience, and Treason

This essay relates part of Helmut's Army story from a different perspective.

Imagine yourself in training at the Signal Corps of the Army of the United States. It is February 1945 and you are stationed in Missouri or some other godforsaken part of the country. You are asked to install an antenna on top of a 90 foot high telephone pole. To do this you must strap spikes on your boots and wear a long belt around your waist and the pole. If you lean away from the pole, the spikes will dig into the wood allowing you to climb.

So far, so good. But high up on the pole your instinct will tell you to cling to the pole for dear life. At that point, the spikes no longer dig into wood and you will descend rather speedily. You may then find yourself back on earth, but with broken bones. If you are lucky, you will not break your bones, but will look like a porcupine with hundreds of wooden splinters adorning you.

To tell the truth, climbing this pole never appealed to me. At thirty feet up I balked like a stubborn mule. I would climb no higher. Call it fear or cowardice; I call it common sense. I realized that the Signal Corps and I were not made for each other. We had come to a falling out once before when they rejected me for training as a telegraph repair man because, being somewhat color blind, I could not tell the difference between the color-coded wires that the telegraph devices required. Today, I would probably sue them for discrimination.

Fortunately about that time, I heard from a former schoolmate of mine from Hamburg that he was stationed at a Military Intelligence Training Camp, Camp Ritchie, Maryland, in the Blue Ridge Mountains and that he loved it. He could not tell me details, but suggested that I apply for a transfer. I looked up "military intelligence" in a dictionary because it seemed like an oxymoron. To tell the truth, never in my life had I met so many dunderheads as in the Army. But the dictionary also told me the MI could mean "obtaining secret information."

This appealed to me. I saw myself as a spy infiltrating Hitler's armies and passing important matters to the armies of the U.S. Even if caught and shot like Mata Harie, it would have been a nobler death than becoming a fatality at the bottom of a telephone pole.

I followed my friend's advice and made out seemingly endless forms requesting a transfer, but nothing happened. I might as well have petitioned a statue. In desperation, I then sent a short letter to the adjutant at Camp Ritchie, a Lt. Colonel by the name of Mary Jones. It began "Dear Ms. Jones" and went on to say that I was not happy in the Signal Corps and that I would be more useful to the Army if I could make use of my fluency in German sowould she please request my transfer.

One should never underestimate the power of a woman: A week later I was called into the office of the commandant and was given orders to report to Camp Ritchie. If I had thought that he would express sorrow at my leaving, I was mistaken. He didn't shed a tear. I saluted smartly and packed my duffel bags.

At the time it was to be a closely guarded secret, but now it can be told: Camp Ritchie was a training center for German speaking soldiers, mostly former refugees. We were trained to interview German prisoners of war. The interviews would take place close to the battle lines to obtain fresh information to help General Headquarters in their battle plans. To conduct these interviews with some finesse, we had to learn the makeup of the German Army from the ground on up, to identify their uniforms, the size of their squadrons, companies, battalions, etc. In the end I knew the composition of their Army as well or better than as any of their generals.

To tell the truth, though, I was a bit disappointed that this would be a rather prosaic occupation, not to be a cloak and dagger assignment I had hoped for. To compensate for this was the prospect that at the end of our training we would be sent to an officer candidate school to become officers, if not gentlemen.

Now comes the hitch that I've been eager to tell you about all along: During a brief furlough I went to New York City. Among other things to see, I dropped in to see the Rockettes at Radio City, a delight to any soldier who had not seen so many beautiful ladies and their legs for years. I was the only soldier in the midst of many women in the audience. At some point in the show the Master of Ceremonies, cheerfulness and good will oozing from him, with microphone in hand, said he was pleased to see a soldier and asked me to step up on stage. I did so, somewhat bashfully. There was a bit of chitchat, then the question: "Where are you stationed?" I told him; I had no trouble with that. But then he said he had never heard of Camp Ritchie. "What kind of outfit is that?"

This really stunned me. For a month or more I had been drilled never to mention military intelligence to anyone. And now, was I to divulge this secret to millions of Americans who were listening to this program on their radios? How would President Roosevelt react if he heard me utter these treasonable words? The very least I could expect was a court martial, years in jail, and a dishonorable discharge.

On the other hand, I had been brought up to always tell the truth. I also remembered

reading "Lying" by Cecily Bok. She disapproved of lying except if it was to save someone's life. What she forgot was that now the life to be saved was my own. I hesitated. The questioning eyes of the Master of Ceremonies were upon me. Then I came to a decision. "Infantry," I finally blurted out. The Master of Ceremonies thanked me, expressed gratitude for all the good soldiers who, like myself, were ready to die for their country, then lead the audience to a roaring applause.

On my return to Camp Ritchie I received orders to report to an officer training school at Fort Benning. It was – you guessed it – the largest infantry camp in the United States.

Chapter 6

Civilian Again, Service in Asia

After my discharge from the Army in August 1946, I stayed another year in Japan working as a civil servant in Tokyo at the Economic Research Bureau of General MacArthur's Headquarters. I was 25. My job title was "Economic Analyst, grade 7," a fancy title but about as appropriate as calling a garbage collector an environmental engineer. I had never been interested in economics, had not studied it, and was ignorant of what an economic analyst did. I was hired because there were only a few U.S. civilians in Japan at the time. Just knowing my ABC's would have gotten me the job.

I was billeted in Tokyo in the same hotel where I had stayed upon first arriving in Japan. Every morning I walked to the nearby office of the Economic Research department, which reported to GHQ, General MacArthur's Headquarters. Even the civil service was still part of the army of occupation. The earthquake resistant Imperial Hotel built by Frank Lloyd Wright in the 1920s, and now occupied by the General and his staff, was close by. I shared an office with about half a dozen Americans and a few English-speaking Japanese interpreters. Only the head of the department, a genuine economist, had a room of his own.

I soon lost my fear that I would not qualify for the job, for my duties were simple: Once a month, representatives from various Japanese industries had to report to me how much their factories had produced. Was this information accurate? During the war, their factory managers had been so used to publishing wildly optimistic figures to please the military that we suspected they continued this practice under the American occupation. But, accurate or not, my coworkers and I published the information as we received it in monthly bulletins. These showed a slowly reviving the Japanese economy which had come to a near stand-still at the end of the war. If our reports were a bit inflated, we didn't mind; we all genuinely wanted Japan to recover.

The industry representatives often invited us to their factories. Perhaps they expected concessions from us, but if they did, they came to the wrong department. We neither had the power nor the desire to meddle in their affairs. Once, a car maker invited us to look at a start-up of a huge assembly line bought from the United States just before the war. Little did we dream that the cars rolling off this and other assembly lines would, in years to come, often outnumber our own.

I welcomed these breaks in the daily routine, since the visits often included lavish, company sponsored dinners, replete with sake and kimono clad, and beautiful geisha girls to refill our cups. They filled these small, cups so frequently that it was only later when we tried to get up that we noticed that the room had begun to dance around us.

The lavish dinners contrasted starkly with to the poverty that we saw all around us, such as the poor waiting in line outside the Army mess halls to receive leftover food. Even the middle class suffered. Our department, for instance, employed several well-educated, English-speaking, now impoverished Japanese clerks to whom we sometimes gave packages of food to take home to their families. In typical Japanese style they would thank us by bowing so many times that it made us wince. Strangely, I don't recall seeing beggars on the street. Only small children often accosted us for much craved chocolate and sweets.

I continued friendships with several people I had known while in uniform. Among them was a captain in the Indian Army, an American doctor, and American civilian women who had come to Japan to work and perhaps to seek adventure and romance. With these friends, I often left Tokyo to enjoy weekends in the country. We travelled either in the captain's jeep or by train. The front of the train, reserved for the Japanese, was often so overcrowded that people clung to the top of the carriages. By contrast, attached to the rear, we traveled for free in often half empty cars. I must admit that we enjoyed these and other privileges of the occupation with little shame or guilt.

In the winter, we went skiing in the Japanese Alps at Shiga Heights – one of the most beautiful regions of the country. When we arrived at night after a two hour train ride, a half-track vehicle waited to take us on snow-covered roads to a posh hotel taken over by the occupation forces. We went sledding and I, not very successfully, tried to learn to ski without looking like a scarecrow in a storm.

During the warmer seasons, we often went on weekend day trips or stayed overnight at inns. We slept on futons that we rolled up and stashed away by day. The center of the bedroom contained a shallow depression for a hibachi, a charcoal burner. On cool nights, we grouped around it like spokes of a wheel, our feet pointing to the glowing coal. Though, by order of General MacArthur, Japanese inns were off limits to Americans, the law was easy to evade. We took K-rations along (prepackaged army food), disdained by us, cherished by the Japanese. We exchanged them for native dishes of rice and fish.

I delighted in these escapes from the city. I loved the beauty of the country with its terraced cultivated hills. I loved the quietness and simplicity of life, even the smell of 'honey buckets' full of manure. I especially loved the Japanese homes; wood-framed, covered with translucent rice paper, light, airy, and sparsely furnished with understated elegance. (To my dismay, I recently read that Japan has begun to import American prefabricated houses.)

I regret that I never learned Japanese language beyond counting to ten, saying hello, or asking for a refill in restaurants. Because of this, and because the non-fraternization laws made social contacts difficult, I never fully understood the Japanese. They seemed friendly enough, but did they really like us? It was hard to know what they really felt. I couldn't decide. I prefer politeness to rudeness, of course, but felt their politeness excessive and a barrier to sincerity. I was also strangely ambivalent about their women. Instead of laughing outright, they giggled and simpered and bashfully covered their mouths. On the other hand, like many American men, I was attracted to them by their being so very feminine. Many American men shared this feeling. Scorning the non-fraternization laws, they not only lived with Japanese girls, but married them and took their brides back to the States. I sometimes wonder whether they ever stopped saying, "oh, my aching back," a phrase (and often the only English) they had picked up from American boy soldiers.

In early August, 1947, my one year civil service appointment came to an end, and I prepared to return to the United States. I wanted to take advantage of the so-called G.I. Bill, a government program offering a free college education to any serviceman or servicewoman for the same length of time they had served. I was accepted at the University of Wisconsin, my home state. Since I had about a month left before the beginning of the

Fall semester, I decided not to go back to the States directly but to make a detour to China, about 1,200 miles South West of Tokyo – roughly the distance between New York and Miami.

Crossing the China Sea on a large passenger ship took about two uneventful days. Though I carried at most a hundred American dollars in paper money with me, my lifetime savings, a savvy fellow passenger warned me that it might be confiscated upon my arrival in Shanghai by Chinese Customs. He suggested that I smuggle it into the country by hiding it in a hollowed bar of soap. In the privacy of my cabin I therefore carefully cut a soap bar in half, hollowed it out, inserted the bills, pressed the halves together and carefully smoothed the seams. This left me proud at my daring, yet scared I might be caught and imprisoned. When I went ashore in China I was inwardly trembling. But a bored customs officer let me pass without even giving me a second look. I was relieved, of course, but also disappointed at having gone to all the trouble for nothing.

In Shanghai, I got in touch with the Komor family whose name and address had been given to me by a friend of theirs. They were Jewish refugees from Hungary who had been interned by the Japanese during the war. They invited me to their house and I stayed with them for a few days. They were very hospitable. And yet, poking around Shanghai for a few days I soon got bored by this sprawling, all too Western metropolis. I decided to push on to the more ancient and romantic sounding Beijing.

To pay for my plane tickets, I first had to exchange my American bills, still smelling of soap, for Chinese dollars. Because of rampant inflation, I would have been foolish to do this legally at the outrageously unfair official rate. The Komors therefore kindly offered to exchange about $40 of my money on the black market. Soon they returned with a sizable suitcase filled with about twenty thousand Chinese dollars, neatly tied into twenty bundles of hundred dollar bills. I began to count the bills in each bundle, but the Komors assured me that I didn't have to because the airline would not count them either. As long as everyone accepted these bundles at face value, they said, the system worked just fine! And they were right! At the airline counter I dumped the contents of my suitcase on the counter, they counted the bundles, and issued the ticket in minutes.

Beijing lies about 600 miles north-northwest of Shanghai. The plane flew so high and the cloud covers were so dense that I could only glimpse isolated patches of the mountains and valleys below me. When we landed in Beijing, I checked into one of the western hotels and then went sightseeing.

At the hotel's entrance I was immediately besieged by dozens of shouting, arm-waving rickshaw men vying to be my guide. I settled on one man in his early 30's and had no reason to regret it. He knew only a few English words but made up for this lack by his friendliness, his knowledge of the city, and his endurance to pull the heavy rickshaw at a steady trot. He was a married man with two children. Once, when I had torn my trousers, he took them home to have his wife mend them. I did not see his home, but once, in the poorer part of the city, he pointed to its gate set in a stone wall. I liked him, and always felt it wasn't right that I should be the master and he the slave.

My memory of Beijing has faded. But I do remember that I felt that now, indeed, I had arrived in the real China, the land of ancient palaces, temples, pagodas, huge gates, massive walls, mud shacks, hotels, streets crowded with vendors, beggars, throngs of people walking, or whizzing by on bicycles or rickshaws, the noise, the smells of cars, shouts by vendors and sporadic Oriental music. I set out in my rickshaw one morning at dawn to see elephants bringing coal into the city, only to be disappointed when, on that particular day, they did not come. The other memory is of stifling heat in my non air conditioned room. In desperation, I tried to sleep in my bathtub filled with cold water, but I do not recommend it.

I stayed in Beijing for three or four days and then decided to fly back to Shanghai. It was now the middle of August and I wanted to be back in the States early in September in time for the Fall semester at the University of Wisconsin. But I had not kept up with the news. I did not know that Communists armies were closing in on to the city. Many wanted to flee before this happened and all flights out of the city were booked for weeks in advance. My best and perhaps only chance to get to Shanghai was to detour by train to Tientsin on the coast, miles from Beijing.

Half an hour after my train left the Beijing station, it came to a screeching halt. What was the cause? Startled, I looked out of the window but saw only a peaceful countryside studded with rice fields. I was puzzled, as were my fellow passengers. Several left the train to find out what had happened. When they returned, an English speaking man told me that nearby Communist troops had blown up the tracks at night, a common happening that the train crews knew how to deal with. Within a few hours, they had repaired the rails. We proceeded to Tientsin without incident.

I had thought that it would be easy to book a flight from Tientsin to Shanghai because Tientsin did not seem to be in danger of an imminent Communist takeover. (About a year later the Communists defeated the Nationalists and took over all of mainland China.) I was mistaken, however. As in Beijing, flights out of the city were booked for weeks in advanced. Looking at my calendar, I became quite anxious. I wanted to be in Madison,

Wisconsin by September to enroll at the University; it was now mid-August. To get advice, I went to Tientsin's popular country club for foreigners. Though the members were friendly and allowed me to use their swimming pool, they could not help me to quickly get back to the States. As a last resort I went to the American Consulate and pleaded my case. I must have pleaded well. One of their vice consuls gave me permission to fly on one of their single engine planes that would take mail to Shanghai the next day.

Flying over China in a somewhat rickety, old, single engine plane was not something I would ordinarily have savored, but under the circumstances I gratefully accepted the consul's offer. As I had expected, the flight was slow, uncomfortable, and bumpy. At times I wished I had been given a parachute. But at least it got me back to Shanghai.

Nowadays, I would surely have taken a plane to return to the States. But 50 years ago, travel by ship was still the more common way to cross the ocean, especially for an almost broke youngster like myself. I booked passage on a freighter, having been told that not only were they cheaper than passenger ships, but also more fun, and that the few passengers they took on got the same accommodations and privileges as the ship's officers.

What I hadn't been told was that freighter schedules are not written in stone. Their published tables of arrival and departure are often figments of some shipping clerk's imagination, or, at best an expression of his wishful thinking. Our freighter was not an exception. Only three other passengers were on board. The ship was to take us to New York City via the Panama Canal after a short layover in the Philippine Islands. We were already sailing toward Manila when the captain assembled the four of us and blithely announced that he had been ordered to change course and take us to New York via Singapore, Malaya, the Indian Ocean, the Suez Canal, the Mediterranean Sea, and the Atlantic Ocean. In other words, to sail West rather than East. The only thing left of the original schedule was New York City.

I now faced a difficult decision: I could get off the ship in Manila and try to get passage from there to San Francisco and perhaps arrive in Madison in good time, or, without having to pay any more than my original ticket price, stay with the freighter, see more of the Orient, perhaps visit the pyramids while the freighter slowly traveled through the Suez Canal, but likely arrive late for winter registration.

In the end it was one of the passengers, a young, attractive woman that made me decide. We had become fond of each other and she confided in me the difficult decision she had to make. She had said good-bye to a young man in Shanghai who had since then besieged her with almost daily cables to marry him. He wanted her to stay on the freighter but get off in Singapore and rejoin him in Shanghai. She liked him, but did she love him? To that question to which she had no answer.

Since she opted to stay on the freighter, I did too, hoping that she would not let herself be persuaded by the young man in Shanghai. I imagined him as exceedingly unattractive in both character and looks. Alas, this monster of a man, unbeknown to us, had flown from Shanghai to Singapore on the southern tip of the Malayan Peninsula to await her arrival. What is a girl to say to such devotion? How could she resist? She left the ship. For me, her leaving and wandering off with the man spelled pure misery.

While the freighter stopped in Singapore for two days to take on heaven only knows what kind of cargo, I moped around the teeming, hot, smelly city. Jealously, I kept thinking of the girl and the man. Quite unreasonably, I felt betrayed. I was glad when the freighter lifted anchor to sail along the western coast of the Malayan Peninsula.

I felt alone and crabby. The cabin was hot and stuffy. My cabin mate and I, a man in his 30's who had worked for the United Nations, got on each other's nerves. I was also angry with Neptune, the Roman god of the oceans. He either blew huge waves that made me sick; or he would rest and bore me as I stood at the rails, overlooking vast expanses of placid water. How deceptive, I thought, were the travel ads showing happy couples on sunny decks. Where, oh where, was the romance of the Far East? I felt imprisoned on the ship, and nostalgic when reminiscing of my two years in Japan. The heat was stifling. I continued to be a grouch most of the way to New York.

Let me fast forward to get some of these depressing days behind me. We sailed along the West coast of the Malaysian Peninsula to the port of Kelang. The freighter stopped there for a few days to take on cargo, probably copra. I took a bus through rain forest and rubber plantations to Kuala Lumpur, Malaya's Capital.- Big city, boring, half a million people, mostly Chinese. I returned to ship. We sailed west through the Bay of Bengal, past the southern tip of India, on through the Arabian Sea to Aden near the entrance of the Red Sea. We sailed on to the entrance of the Suez Canal. I had hoped to go ashore to see the pyramids while the ship slowly chugged its way through the 100 mile long Canal, but I wasn't allowed to because of a cholera outbreak in Egypt. It was very hot and humid. I was still out of sorts and worried about being late for registration at the University of Wisconsin.

When we arrived at Port Said where the Canal meets the Mediterranean, my cabin mate and I were idling on deck when we saw a merchant in a row boat tie up alongside our ship. The boat owner, a friendly, good looking Egyptian man in his 20's, climbed aboard on a rope ladder, pointed to several whiskey cases in his boat and offered to sell these to us at about half of stateside prices. I cursed myself for being nearly broke. My cabin mate, however, more flush than I, decided to take advantage of the bargain. But he was no sucker: Foreseeing the possibility that the young merchant might simply take the money and abscond, he insisted on a guarantee before paying. The young Egyptian seemed to understand his caution and readily agreed to leave a safety deposit. He pulled a gold ring off his hand - it seemed to be his wedding ring - to exchange for the money, then then went down the ladder to get the whiskey. Or so we thought! The last we saw of him, he was rowing away toward the coast as fast as he could.

"How strange," my roommate mused, "He left his gold ring – surely worth more than the whiskey."

"Not so," said a passing crew member who had witnessed the last part of the transaction.

"You've been had. It's an old trick around here. You just bought yourself a gilded ring worth about a dime." "The merchant," he added, "did not think himself a thief (his religion would forbid that), since he had given at least something for the money he had received."

Morality, after all, is relative. Then we sailed west. New York was now only about a week away.

When I glimpsed at the Statue of Liberty on the distant horizon, I suddenly felt a rush of love for this country. Only the day before, nostalgic about my years in Asia, I had thought of the United States only as a vast, undefinable continent. I had arrived there as a refugee some six years ago and had often felt then, that I was an observer from Europe, an alien, not quite assimilated.

Returning now, I was and felt like an American citizen, proud of his country. It was the best in the world, the land of opportunity and equality. However, a more critical voice in me whispered that opportunity did not exist for all, that equality was at best a dream, that big corporations had too much power, and that politicians were often corrupt. And yet, I was still grateful that in this country I could at least voice my concerns, try to make things better, and vote without fear of retribution.

Something else cheered me – I had been raised by parents who had a high school education, were reasonably intelligent, but whose interests, perhaps understandably, were focused mainly on making a living. At home, in Germany, as well as later in America, I heard next to nothing about either the sciences or the humanities. My coworkers and the few friends I had did nothing to fill this vacuum either. Fortunately, something in me, perhaps just plain curiosity, had made me start to read. I read almost at random – biographies, essays on architecture, 19th century literature, scientific news, even detective stories. But there was then nobody to reinforce my interests or to direct them. As I stepped ashore in New York in September, 1947, I was therefore thrilled at the prospect of continuing the university education that I had begun two years earlier when I was still a soldier. I hoped the university would help me put together the bits and pieces of information and wisdom that had come my way and, perhaps equally important, help me find a profession. My eyes were on the future, and the future looked good.

From New York I flew to Milwaukee, Wisconsin, and stopped briefly to visit my parents whom I had not seen for two years. I had mixed feelings about the reunion, having been on my own and, thank you, doing very well during my life abroad. I then took a bus to Madison, the site of the University of Wisconsin. I arrived there just in the nick of time to register for the Fall, one among thousands, many of them returning veterans. Like me, they were taking advantage of the so-called GI Bill of rights. The Bill stipulated that any veteran could study at government expense for a period equal to the time of his or her service in the Armed Forces. This meant that my fees would be paid for three years, long enough to get a bachelor's degree. A good deal, indeed. (Today, even at State Universities, these fees would amount to several tens of thousands of dollars. My record shows that, by contrast, the total cost the Veterans Administration paid for my education between 1947 and the date of my graduation in 1950, was only $930.72 plus $202.82 for books! But remember, wages were low.)

One could usually tell a veteran from a non-veteran undergraduate. Usually he was male, older, and, if not battle scarred, a bit wiser in the ways of the world. He was not likely to belong to a fraternity, in fact looked at them with disdain. Strangely, though, he did not usually bond with other veterans.

Chapter 7

Student Years - College and Graduate School

Though I have not visited the University of Wisconsin since I left it in 1951, I remember it with nostalgia. The three years or so I spent there were among the happiest in my life.[29] Part of this was because of the attractiveness of the campus. Later, I saw many campuses, but I still think that the U of W was the prettiest. Many students came from out of state, mostly New York, probably attracted by the beauty of the setting as much as I was.

The university borders on Lake Mendota, which, lovely in itself, also sets a desirable, natural limit to the city of Madison's growth and keeps if from swallowing up the University. From the window of my Kronshage dormitory, less than a hundred feet from the lake, I would often watch the students canoeing during the summer and skating in the winter. Close by, also on the lake, was the large student union, the center of student activity. I not only ate my meals there, but spent much of my free time watching a movie, listening to a talk, in the music room, or snacking and chatting in the cafeteria. The cafeteria opened to a terrace where one could sit in the summer and relax. It differed from other student unions in that had its own boathouse and, a rarity in those days, sold beer. Perhaps the bar had a pipeline from the beer factories in nearby Milwaukee. In any case, though not a beer drinker myself, I thought the selling of beer as a sign of Wisconsin's liberalism. I never saw any drunks; they probably holed up in the sororities and fraternities. Next to the cafeteria was the boathouse where we could rent canoes for romantic (or just friendly) dates.

I wish my mother could have understood my enjoyment of the beauty of the campus and its social life, but she was dismayed to hear that I spent most of my time going to classes and doing my homework. This was student life? From seeing German movies dealing with nineteenth century university life, she had come to expect that students were always in the throes of torrid love affairs, getting happily drunk in the Rathskellers, or fighting duels.

I have always been curious. I am glad I was; I still am. I think it is curiosity that sets us apart from animals, that makes us tick with a different tune. My years at the university now gave me opportunities to stuff my hungry, undernourished mind with facts and ideas. The many courses I saw listed in the school bulletin attracted me like a smorgasbord table laden with delicacies.

I was also pleased to have a clearly defined, fairly easily achievable goal in mind: I was to obtain 120 credits in three years. That was the minimum that I wanted to achieve. Beyond that, I also wanted to do well in my classes and to prepare myself for a professional career.

But how was I to choose what courses to take, what field to major in? Just about every course sounded interesting! After stewing over this for a while, I decided to major in physics, but to squeeze in as many humanities courses as I could. In this way, I felt I could have the best of both worlds: the world of science, where it might be easier to find a job, and the world of literature and philosophy, which I felt would be more entertaining and fulfilling.

During my senior year, I even thought of combining these two fields by becoming a science journalist. I therefore enrolled in a journalism course on writing feature articles. In some ways, this was a fun relief from the more difficult physics, chemistry, and biology courses that I was taking, but the instructor had us waste too much time studying magazine ads. She reasoned that every journal article should be addressed or slanted toward a specific reader and that the targeted readership of any publication could best be determined by studying the ads between its covers. This was all very well and good, but anything can be overdone!

What I found more useful was her telling us to, "keep your feature nose out at all times." She had us walk along main streets, our "feature noses" out front, to find suitable ideas for feature articles. I found several, one about a coop housing project shared by white and black students. I headlined the article "The House of Many Colors." I got an A for this, as well as for the final course grade, but never had anything published. Not discouraged, I wrote to several magazines and newspapers asking for employment as a science writer, but received no responses. I have no regrets. I thought at the time that being a science writer meant being on the forefront of new discoveries. Today, I see science writers more as parasites picking other people's brains. Is this sour grapes, or is it a genuine evaluation? I leave it as a question.

The lecturer I admired most was a woman who taught Biology I to an audience of hundreds. She would start every lecture exactly on the hour, speak quickly, beautifully, and concisely for one hour without notes, and complete her lecture just at the moment when the bell rang. I admired everything about her: her punctuality, her clear speaking style, and that she always finished her lectures on time.

Berkeley experience . . . needs to be written if it hasn't.[30]

I got my M.A. in Teaching from Harvard's Graduate School of Education in 1952, but I knew by then that I had no calling to be a teacher. During my year at Harvard, I had worked as a teaching assistant at Brandeis University in a science course for liberal arts students. I taught there to supplement my meager income from the Government's G.I. Bill of Rights. I also taught a course in general science at a Waltham High School to satisfy Harvard's requirement for practice teaching.

Both at Brandeis and in Waltham I felt unsure of myself. I was too concerned about the subject matter I had to get across, and not concerned enough about the students. I tried to make the Waltham class as interesting as possible by asking the students to plan to shoot a manned space satellite into orbit to the moon. Sputnik had just been launched, and the topic was therefore hot. The students were to form small teams, each one of which was to come up with solutions as to what kind of fuel was required to launch the spacecraft, what kind of food was to be taken aboard, and how the air was to be replenished. The project was fairly successful, but not enough to want me to teach for the rest of my life.

My experiences at Brandeis and Waltham High convinced me that I lacked the necessary patience with students and was moreover handicapped by my inability to remember their faces. I found later that many people have this handicap, which is known as a medical condition, prosopagnosia. I therefore saw the class, not as individuals but as a fairly homogeneous mass.

In the end, my year at the Harvard Graduate School of Education had been pretty much a waste, except that I could now add an M.A. in Teaching to my credentials.

My three years of study paid for by the G.I. Bill had come to an end. Now I had to find a job. Luckily, the above-mentioned Russian Sputnik caused a great demand for scientists to expand the almost non-existent U.S space program. This was true, even for people like me who had only a B.S degree in physics. I accepted a job offer from the Battelle Memorial Institute in Columbus, Ohio.

Chapter 8

Work Life 1952-1979

My first job after getting my M.A. in Teaching from Harvard Graduate School of Education was with the Battelle Memorial Institute in Columbus, Ohio. This was, and is, a huge research institute, much larger than A.D. Little in Cambridge. Battelle Memorial Institute is a huge research complex with a staff of over seven thousand scientists and engineers engaged in about two thousand projects (2003 figures).

I had no love for my first two assignments. One was to grow a bar of silver chloride from a seed crystal in a specially designed oven, the resulting material having a structure somewhat similar to steel. But, in contrast to steel, being transparent it could be observed and photographed while being tested for fatigue failure. It was hoped that this would produce insight for the failure of steel under repeated stress. I remember seeing machines that, day and night, pounded replicas of human buttocks onto automobile seats to find out how many bounces they could take before breaking. I produced the required silver chloride bars; so corrosive that they etched the metal holders in the testing machine, but do not know what happened to the project. Quite likely, it ended with an inconclusive report.

My second project was sponsored by Corning Glass. They wondered if they could make an aneroid barometer of quartz (instead of the usual bronze) to minimize the effect of hysteresis due to internal friction. These barometers were used in altimeters in airplanes. The effect of hysteresis was that when a plane ascended to a given altitude, the instrument would show a slightly different reading than when the plane descended, evidently an unwelcome effect. The barometer consisted of two corrugated round quartz discs that were fused at their perimeter and evacuated. A change in the external air pressure would then expand or contract the capsule, and the small change was magnified and displayed. Though the idea of substituting quartz for bronze seemed sound, I found that the necessary thickness that was required of the quartz capsule so as not to break made it too insensitive for use as an altimeter. One good thing came out of this project; a trip with my supervisor, Mr. Grover, to Corning Glass in New York State.

After about a year at Battelle, I heard of an opening in the Graphic Arts Department. The graphic arts were, and still are, particularly interesting to me, insofar that they bridge the gap between science and technology, that they involve both physics and chemistry, and that, most important, they have immediate applications. I was fortunate to witness and participate in the early development of Xerography.

Xerography was invented in the 1940's by a scientist who made use of the fact that selenium was an electric insulator in the dark, but a conductor in light. In my kitchen, I coated metal plates with a thin film of selenium and rubbed them with a piece of fur. In darkness, the resulting electrons would sit on the plate's surface, but in light, they would leak away. A positively charged powder sprinkled on the plate would then stick to the electrons, but not to the light-struck parts. The powder could then be transferred to paper and fused. I took my invention to several companies, but was told that if the invention had any commercial value, their own scientists would have developed it.

I was more fortunate with Battelle, who drew up a contract with him to develop my idea. When I joined the team lead by Lewis Walkup, the project had advanced beyond the fur-rubbing stage, and a fair copy of a document could be made in 'as little' as a minute. A variant of the method described above, one especially useful for producing printing plates, was to transfer the image from the selenium onto a metal printing plate attached to a revolving drum. Unfortunately, the powder transfer from the selenium to the printing plate was spotty; a fact that I reasoned came from the powder hopping back and forth between the electrically changed plates. I was able to show that a heating pad under the printing plate resulted in a much-improved transfer since the powder melted on the heated plate and thus, stayed in place.

I received my first patent for this suggestion. After the disappointments with my previous projects, this was a welcome sign that, given the right kind of project and freedom and encouragement from my boss, my contributions were at last valued.[31]

Chapter 9

Marriage & Children

I met Bridget Tancock at the English Speaking Union (ESU) sometime in about 1958. The ESU met once a week at an apartment they rented for the evening from the College Club, then and now near the Public Garden on Commonwealth Ave. in Boston. These were purely social affairs that offered companionship in a relaxed atmosphere and cemented ties between American and English members. Usually, only about 10 attended, most under 40. Coffee or tea and cookies were about the only refreshments available. At the time, I was working for the Electronics Corporation across the river at 1 Memorial Drive in Cambridge. I was about 37 years old, and though I had had a series of more or less intimate (and usually not long lasting) relations with women, I was still single. At close to 40, I felt that it was high time to settle down. At the time I lived in Cambridge, and worked at Technical Operations in Lexington.

Bridget had come to America a few years before to study Sociology from the Harvard Graduate School of Education – the same school I had attended for a year in 1952 to obtain a M.A. in Teaching. I met her and I liked her right away for her naturalness (no makeup, nothing phony), her intelligence (without touting it) and her speech, which struck me as English at its best. At the time she was living with Betty Wyeth and two other women in Cambridge. She had come from England where she was born in Reading in 1928, the oldest of three sisters. Her father, Ernest Tancock, had been a schoolmaster of a boys' school near Reading, but was retired now and lived with his wife, Kitty, in Oxford. Bridget had obtained her bachelor's degree at the London School of Economics, and had afterwards taught at a school in London.[32]

When I met her, Bridget was close to getting an Ed.D. She was working on her thesis . . . trying to find out if, and how, children raised in nuclear families (ie with a man as head of the household) differed from children in non-nuclear families. Our friendship deepened but never became sexual. This was partly because sex had never been the most important factor in a relationship, partly because we lived in pre-Hippie times when sexual license was not flouted as it was a decade later.

We dated for a few months, even went for a weekend to my recently acquired Maine cottage. During this time, she was finishing her thesis. I helped her edit and proofread it. We approached the possibility of marriage rather gingerly at first by discussing how children in a mixed marriage would fare and what difficulties might be expected. As we edged closer to the possibility of marriage, were also concerned how her parents would react, not so much because I was Jewish, but because her father might resent my having come from Germany. He had been gassed by the Germans during WWI, and presumably was not very fond of them for that reason. Fortunately, she need not have worried. He was always kind to me.

We set our wedding date to coincide with Bridget's graduation. After obtaining the necessary license from the City Hall in Cambridge, we were married at the home of a Chinese-American Justice of the Peace. He had been recommended to us as performing weddings for mixed-marriage couples that did not want a church or temple ceremony. I invited a friend, and so did Bridget. Afterwards we went to as small party in Cambridge at the home of Professor John Whiting, Bridget's thesis advisor, and his wife, Bea. (Whiting died in 1999.)

We spent our honeymoon at St. Croix, but also spent a day at St. John and at Monheagan Island. When we returned, we lived in a converted garage on Appleton St., Cambridge. The garage was adjacent to a house belonging to a Mr. Churchill. Previously, I had rented a room in the Churchill's home. The converted garage was rather quaint in that we had to climb a vertical ladder from the first floor to the second that contained the bed and bathroom. By the time we lived there, I think Mr. Churchill had died. I don't remember why, after a few months, we moved to an apartment with the Shurcliff's nearby. Bridget had canvased the neighborhood till she found it. Dr. Shurcliff was a well-known physicist whose specialty was optics, the very field that I was engaged in.

When Bridget got pregnant, we began to look for a house and found one at 84 Goden St. in Belmont. David and Joan were born while we lived there.

In about 1967, we bought the house at 11 Devon Road. These were the best years in my life.

* * *

Note: Perhaps because of his sadness, or just trouble remembering, Helmut had difficulty writing about these times. Zahara suggested the following prompts, but he never completed this section.

Because I was working full time, my memories from the children's early years are fuzzy. However, here are a few recollections:

1. When the children were small we went to England to see Bridget's family. I remember on one of these trips . . .
2. Some of our happiest times were vacations in our cottage in Maine. From those trips, I remember . . .
3. Many Christmases, we went to Canada to Bridget's cousins' Pauline and Alf Best's home in Toronto. I remember . . .
4. In the summer, we sometimes visited Paul and Alf's farm as well. I recall that . . .

* * *

Now came the worst years: First of course, there was the unexpected death of Bridget of breast cancer in 1976. I now became suddenly the sole provider for the children. David was 13, Zahara (then Joan) almost 12, and Rachel not even 10 years old. Rather than feeling this as a burden, I think it helped me to pull myself together. I had no time for self-pity. I also felt some pride that I, already in my 60's, and working 40 hours a week, was still able to cope, with children and a large house to look after. Superficially, the children also seemed to be doing remarkable well, carrying on with school and other daily tasks. Since I worked forty hours a week, I engaged a young woman and later a young man to do some chores like cooking, cleaning the kitchen, and shopping for food in exchange for a small apartment.

I would have liked to talk to the children about Bridget and to share our memories of her. I still do. But my attempts to do that are met with silence, probably because it was too painful for them. In any case, I couldn't very well force them. Even then I feared, rightly as it turned out, that their inability to talk about their mother and to express and share their feelings with each other and me, were likely to cause them great difficulties later in life. I arranged to have them see a psychologist at MIT, but she, too, as far as I know, could not draw them out.

Unwittingly, but not maliciously, I even gave them ammunition to fuel their anger. I hardly ever, for instance, asked them about their grades in school, telling them, as I believed, that grades were not as important as learning, but also not wanting to praise a better student at the expense of their less successful siblings. I had trouble relating to their friends.

Whenever I came home from work, I would find the children's belongings scattered all over the house, and dirty dishes piled up in the kitchen. I repeatedly asked them, and eventually demanded, that they clean up their act. When they responded with passive resistance, I tried issuing ultimatums. These, too, were usually disregarded, leaving them and me angry at each other.

Perhaps the children's' behavior was fairly typical for teenagers. Whereas fledgling birds leave their nest as soon as they can fly, we humans confine them to their home until they finish high school. Their mother might have seen a universality in their silent rebellion, and taken it in stride. It is likely that the children missed her gentle ways. But I took their behavior as a personal attack. For me, it was a no-win situation. My hands were tied. I could not punish them by confining them to the house, nor could I kick them out. I was frustrated and didn't know what to do. Our mutual anger smoldered for years.

Upset by the constant bickering among us, I asked Dr. Jessica Hamman, a psychotherapist to help us. She came to our house for several weeks, but we made the mistake of setting her up as a kind of judge rather than a therapist. The children would present their case, and I mine, each hoping that Dr. Hammann would find the other side guilty of misdemeanor. The result was that Dr. Hammann did not resolve our conflicts.

These were indeed the bad years. The only consolation for me is that they did well in school, had many friends, and did not get addicted to alcohol and other drugs.

Zahara: As far as I know, except for the brief notes below, Helmut did not write much about his life after retirement, which included travel to many countries and classes at the Harvard Institute for Learning in Retirement. He sold the house in Newton and moved, first to Brookline, then to Cambridge. Most importantly, he enjoyed many years of love and companionship (as well as concerts, book discussions, and travel) with his companion and partner Margaret Cain of Brookline.

Chapter 10

Looking Back

What do I see when I look back on my life? What have I learned? What do I regret? Let me start by counting my blessings.

Of these, the greatest was my marriage. It gave me support, a sense of roots, and a way out of the isolation that I had felt as a single man. Though my marriage was cut short by the early death of my wife, I still feel that I am an anchor for my children. Feeling useful, even needed, is important to me. Having survived the children's difficult adolescent years, I am glad we are again a well-functioning family. Next to my children, I value most my friends, most of whom are women.

I have also been lucky never to have lived in poverty, or at least never to have suffered from it. Even in England, where I lived hand to mouth, I was able to live within my means without feeling deprived. And though I arrived in the United States more or less penniless, I have, whether through luck or foresight, found reasonable financial security. For this, I feel grateful.

My debt to America extends beyond financial security to other forms of success perhaps difficult to achieve in other countries. I was, for instance appointed an officer in the Army of the United States shortly after becoming a citizen even though I was not college educated and still rolled my 'r's' in the German way. I am also indebted to having received a college education at government expense. Because of this, I was able to do research in physics and to obtain several patents relating to applied optics.

Even after college, I have continued my education. I have always loved to read, especially Western literature. This has allowed me to enter vicariously into the lives of others and to understand the diversity of human motives. I also like to go lectures, not out of a priggish sense of duty, but for entertainment. Often, I enjoy them more than movies or T.V. In my 70's now, I have been taking courses at the Harvard Institute for Learning in Retirement.[33] In this way, I replenish much that I have forgotten, learn new subjects, and become a more interesting person in the bargain.

Random Thoughts and Proclamations

I am grateful and appreciative of the United States but I am not uncritical. I was strongly opposed, for instance, to our recent wars in Vietnam, the Falkland Islands, and the Gulf, and I decried our support of the Contras in Nicaragua. I also regret the excesses and injustices of capitalism whenever they occur. But my feelings, even for conditions that I deplore, are tempered by my appreciation that I am free to voice my opposition without fear of retaliation.

Though democracy is not a panacea, I can't think of anything better to replace it. Nor do I think that any political system can provide happiness for all; mankind is too diverse in its needs to live in harmony under one roof. Those who envision a utopia with equality and liberty for all don't realize that these ideals are mutually exclusive. Complete liberty would leave little equality; the laws of the jungle would prevail. Complete equality on the other hand, would require stringent restrictions on liberty. We can only strive for workable compromises.

I am usually introspective and serious but can also see the comic aspects of life. My best friends are those who bring out this lighter side. They allay my fear of being considered too intellectual and cold instead of the warm person I prefer to be.

Throughout our lives we are dealt a deck of cards, some good, some not so good, some quite awful. The fortunate ones make the best of even the bad cards. I'm afraid that I haven't always done that and that often I've even played poorly with the good ones. This was especially so when my children were in their teens, the terrible teens, when they were full of rebellion. Instead of expecting this and seeing it as a natural consequence of growing up, I took their rebellion as a personal attack that had to be answered by counterattacks. That, of course, didn't work and resulted in a few miserable years for all of us.

Writing with Helmut in the 3rd person:
The Doubleman Experiment

Note from Zahara: Here Helmut experiments with writing about himself in the third person, as if he had met himself, sometimes referred to as "Doubleman."

Heckscher is now in his mid-seventies. The point was driven home to me the other day when I saw him in his study. An open astronomy book lay on his desk and he was punching numbers into a small calculator. Looking up he smiled at me, his smile conveying both his pleasure in his cleverness and his sense of wonderment. "Look," he said, "I've traveled more than forty three thousand million miles around the sun on Spaceship Earth at a speed of eighteen and a half miles per second."

When I didn't say anything, he added for emphasis, "Just imagine: Forty three, followed by nine zeros miles! Even light, no slouch when it comes to speed, would have taken almost three days to travel that far."

I was not impressed and told him so. I had often wondered how he, looking backwards, regarded his life and what, if any advice he had for his children. It seemed to me, that in my opinion, it wasn't the length of his ride that mattered but the quality of his journey. I therefore asked him what kind of ride he had had.

I thought I saw a flicker of annoyance on his face. Was he perhaps upset that I had not commented on his calculations? He paused a moment.

Then he said, "Excuse me, but I think that's a silly question, or at least a question that has no simple answer. It's as if you had asked me what the weather had been like on my long trip. I would have said that much of the time the weather had been sunny and that I had even enjoyed the rain and the snow." But sometimes," he added, "it was so cold, that I shivered and froze, or the heat seemed almost unbearable."

"Even then," he continued, "I was often able to protect myself by wearing an overcoat and gloves in the winter, and keeping in the shade when it was hot." He paused for a moment, and then said, "That's how I feel about my travels on Spaceship Earth."

"Isn't that a bit of a copout?" I asked.

"Yes," he replied, "quite likely. My difficulty is that, looking back, I don't know how I could have avoided the rough times had I been more adroit." He paused again, then continued. "Let me change the metaphor."

...

Another time, I asked Doubleman about politics. He said that no political system he knew of, past or present, described in books, or put into practice, was fool proof against the greed, power, lust, and stupidity of man. No system as yet conceived could prevent the rascals of all sorts from rising to the top of the heap. The only question was whether to prefer a system that favored equality at the cost of restrictions, or a free society that, in the extreme, would have its only law the law of the jungle. He admitted that he frequently dithered between the two possibilities, siding with the conservatives one day and with the liberals the next.

On one day, to the dismay of his mostly liberal friends, he saw the poor and unemployed as parasites on hardworking folks and responsible, perhaps they had been lazy in school, or spent their money frivolously, for their poverty. On other, more charitable days, he saw the same people transformed into the salt-of-the-earth, like the poster images of the left. He was well aware of this dichotomy and often chided himself for it without, however, finding a satisfactory solution. As a result, when it came to politics, Heckscher remained a cynic, and a fence sitter.

It is probable that his later cynicism was self-protective. As a rule, he despised cynics, and liked Oscar Wilde's definition that a cynic was a man who knew the price of everything and the value of nothing. In his youth, he had subscribed to the Nation, a liberal magazine, but had become so upset at its weekly exposes of wrongdoing in our society that he canceled his subscription. Ever since then, he had found it better to laugh than to cry.

He was fond of a passage in Somerset Maugham's "Of Human Bondage," that said all life long, one weaved a carpet whose design one could not see until the end. "Well," he said, laughing, "I don't see much design yet. I guess I still have some weaving to do." One section of the carpet, however, was almost completed. It was, he said, a large checkered design that stretched along its length. Most of its colors were muted, but a few stood out in bright, vivid hues.

He would never have become a great physicist. He had never aspired to become one and he did not regret this. His mathematical education and ability, often so very important in this profession, had stopped at elementary calculus and he had never even found much use for that. He downplayed his lack of mathematical ability by saying that mathematicians usually have to make so many simplifying assumptions in their calculations, that the results hardly ever square with reality. Deep down, however, he had to admit to himself that lack of mathematical ability was nothing one should brag about.

He also lacked ambition, considering his twenty years or so of working in research laboratories as nothing much more than making a moderately interesting nine to five living. Most of the projects he worked on were handed down to him from management that had been awarded a profitable government contract. Just as one does not look into a gift horse's mouth, prudent management presumably did not ask if this contract made any sense, and neither did the bench coolie, the scientist who had to carry it to fruition. Even if one makes allowance for the fact that research by its very nature does not always result in useful information or devices, many of the research projects that Heckscher worked on were ill conceived. As a result, he often worked on projects that neither advanced the state of science nor were likely to make this a better world.

In the 1960's, for instance, he spent months on an Air Force contract analyzing light reflected by the earth by aerial reconnaissance. At the end of that time he found that a prism used in the plane's scanner (not designed by him) had been sensitive to the light's polarization, thus invalidating all the data. Many other ill-conceived projects such as an infrared scanning device, a resonance scattering filter, the use of silver chloride to study metal fatigue, using quartz instead of glass for aneroid barometers, and various interferometers come to mind. The reports of these and other ill-conceived projects are now collecting dust in the archives of long forgotten government agencies.

The only projects that really interested Heckscher and which, to him, meant more than bread and butter, were projects that he himself had originated. False modesty often makes him shy of calling himself an inventor, but, as far as his work was concerned, inventiveness was his saving grace. According to Heckscher, most scientists think linearly, going from A to B to C. Inventors tend to jump from A to C or even, if they are good, from A to Z. Great men like Newton, Darwin, and Einstein, manage to do both. Some scientists put down inventors by calling them prima donnas always looking for an ego trip. That may be true, says Heckscher, but what's wrong if the trip is pleasurable and often results in useful discoveries?

Back to First Person

As an agnostic, I hold a difficult position. On the one hand, I doubt that someone named God created the universe. On the other hand, I don't think that even the greatest cosmologists have discovered the 'ultimate truth' or that it will ever be revealed to us. They tell us, and conventional wisdom accepts it, that the universe started with a big bang. But any child might well ask what came before that. My own view, unsatisfactory as it may be, is that human brains are well adapted to serve human needs, just as dog brains serve the needs of dogs. But, just as dogs and other 'lower' animals are kept by their brains from grasping certain niceties of our universe, so our brains are likewise restricted.

I am also skeptical concerning the evolution of life. Here, too, I feel caught between two views neither of which I can accept: creationism on one hand, Darwinism on the other. Even a flea, seen through a microscope is exquisitely complex. I maintain that so far there is no evidence that he and other critters, not to mention man, were made by a supernatural being or have accidentally evolved from primeval slime.

But I don't lose sleep worrying about the origin of the universe or the evolution of life; nor does my agnosticism and skepticism make me a less moral person. The latter, whether inborn or cultural, exists in me and others who believe neither in God or science.

I referred to some successes in my life and that I am not unmindful of my blessings. Sometimes, however, like Walter Mitty in the James Thurber story, I dream of having lived a different life, to have become a famous North Pole explorer, or perhaps another Einstein. Better still, I might have become James Bond agent '007,' who never failed at anything. Though I don't take those dreams seriously, I cannot completely banish them.

Sometimes, I also hear a small but persistent voice that whisper, "You could have achieved more had you been more diligent and ambitious." I cannot deny that charge. For too much of my life, I have acted on a belief that "real men," the "macho men" of today, should succeed without working by the sweat of their brows. Perhaps it was a subliminal message from my mother. But whether it was or not, it has not been a good one to live by.

In my next life, therefore, I will work harder. I will be more attuned to my feelings. I will make a greater effort not only to help my children and my friends, but to make this a better world for all.

Photographs

Helmut as a baby with "Mutti," his mother. Mutti was born Friederike Leipziger (known as "Frieda" or "Friedel") in Jauer, which was then part of Germany and is now in Poland (Jawor). Her parents were Max and Henriette (Bacher) Leipziger. The Leipzigers had a brewery and liquor store. Frieda met Max Heckscher when he came to the store, probably when he was on a sales trip. They married in 1917.

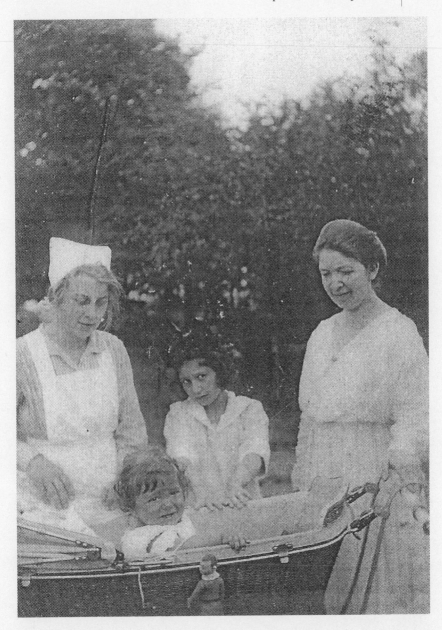

Helmut as a baby with his aunt Else Goldstein (known as "Miez"), who was his mother Frieda's sister; Meiz's daughter Rita Goldstein Oschinsky, who was Helmut's cousin; and Helmut's baby nurse. In 1935, Rita moved to Palestine. Meiz eventually joined her there, but did not like Palestine and settled in the US. (See details in footnote about Rita and her family.)

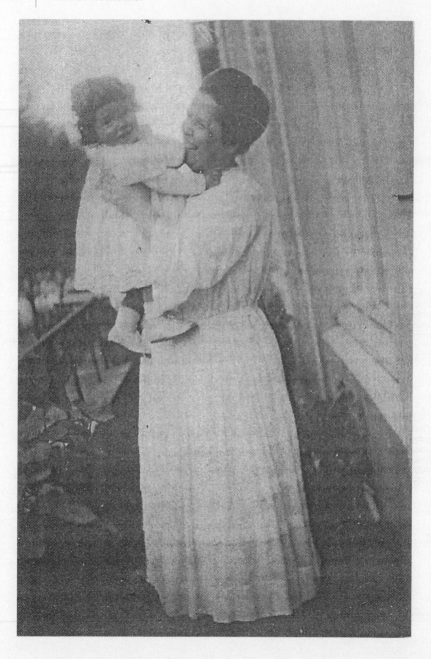

Helmut with Rosa Hoga, in Hamburg, circa 1922. Rosa was the family's cook and maid. She later moved to Milwaukee with the help of Max Heckscher. In 1939, she helped the Heckscher family escape from the Nazis.

Catherine Bridget Tancock and Helmut Heckscher were married in Cambridge, Massachusetts in the home of a Justice of the Peace in Boston. The date coincided with Bridget's graduation.

Helmut, David, Zahara (then Joan) and Rachel hiking on the Appalachian Trail, near Liberty Springs Campsite in White Mountain National Forest in New Hampshire, circa 1977.

APPENDICES

Article from The Milwaukee Journal regarding Rosa Hoga saving the Heckschers

Repays Old Kindness, Saves Jewish Family From Reich
Former Maid Has Her Turn
She's Catholic, and Knew Persecution, Too;
Bond of Friendship 20 Years Old
Kindness Repaid, Family is Saved

Printed May 10, 1939

This is the story of friendship – a friendship that grew through 20 turbulent postwar years into a bond that defied man made laws and pulled three people from the slough of despond 4,000 miles away.

It is the story of the friendship of the Jewish Heckscher family of Hamburg, Germany and their one-time maid, Rose Hoga, a Catholic of Milwaukee.

Begun in the bitter years when inflation was wrecking what was left of war torn Germany, it reached a joyous climax here Tuesday night when Rose welcomed her former employers to Milwaukee, freed by her efforts from Nazi persecution of their race.

He Helped Her Out

Back in the early twenties when Rose was a maid in the well-furnished Heckscher home and Herr Heckscher's clothing business employed 200 men, inflation ate into her lifelong savings, threatening to wipe them out.

Kindly, Herr Heckscher converted what was left into American dollars thus salvaging a substantial sum. Rose decided to turn to the land of her new money and sailed to the United States. She established herself in Milwaukee as a cook.

She never lost touch with the Heckschers. Frequent letters were exchanged and every year cards from Rose marked the birthdays of Herr and Frau Heckscher and their son Helmut.

In 1934, a year after, Hitler came into power. Rose yearned again for her homeland. With her American earnings she bought a confectionary shop in Danzig and settled down to a shopkeeper's placid existence. She visited the Heckschers in Hamburg. The baby Helmut whom she had helped to rear was now a strapping lad in his teens. Over coffee and cakes they laughingly recalled the trials of the postwar years.

Persecution is Begun

But already, rumblings of another sort were threatening to make that ordeal pale in comparison. In Danzig, Nazis began persecution of the strong Catholic population as well as Jews Store windows were smashed, houses painted, people insulted on the street.

Rose remembered the United States where people could live and worship in peace. She sold her store and sailed back to America. German currency regulations forbade her to take any money with her so she left it in the care of her good friends, the Heckschers.

When she left, the Jewish persecutions were rising to a grim crescendo. "If you need help, let me know," she told the Heckschers.

The Heckscher clothing plant found it harder and harder to obtain cloth for its machines. Sales fell off as the pressure on Jews increased. From 200, the firm's employees dropped to 20. Helmut was excluded from school. It would be impossible for him to get either an education or a job in the new Germany.

To Concentration Camp

Finally, last November, Herr Heckscher, now 60, was hustled off to a concentration camp in the purges that followed the shooting of a German embassy secretary in Paris by a Polish Jew.

Rose in Milwaukee heard of the Heckschers' plight. She went to a travel agency with $1,000, the fruit of her years of toil, to try to buy passage to America for her sore pressed friends.

But there were immigration restrictions, refugee regulations and other obstacles. Rose enlisted the aid of Harry Bragarick, Milwaukee volunteer labor dispute mediator. Between them they arranged for the Heckschers' entry into the United States.

Then, Frau Heckscher had to file an application for her husband's release from the concentration camp. He had to agree to the sale, or "Aryanization," of his business. Only a small fraction of his money could leave the Reich. Through the intervention of Rose, Bragarnick and the American consul, Herr Heckscher was released from the concentration camp and given permission to leave Germany.

A Joyous Reunion

Early Tuesday, Herr and Frau Heckscher arrive in Milwaukee, roused Rose and staged a joyous reunion. Tuesday night, they celebrated in true German fashion at the home of Harry Bragarnick. Helmut, now 17, remained in England, where he has a job as research assistant in a chemical laboratory.

"The United States is a wonderful country. Milwaukee is a beautiful city and Rose, oh, such a wonderful friend," the Heckschers exclaimed Wednesday.

But even here an ominous cloud still hovers over them.

"As I left the concentration camp the commandant spoke," Herr Heckscher said. "He said we must forget everything we had seen or experienced in the camp. 'If you breathe one word about it in foreign land, vengeance will be taken on your brothers in Germany,' he told us. 'And don't think that we won't know what you say because the foreign branch of the Nazi party is now so extensive and well organized that we know what is said in every land. Wherever you go our ears will be listening.'"

Translation of life summary of Max Heckscher (1878-1963) by Helmut Heckscher

Translation of a 'life summary' my father, Max Heckscher, wrote on 30 November 1955; at 2905 N. Marietta Ave. Milwaukee, WI. (Helmut Heckscher)

I was born on 7 June 1878 in Hamburg. My father owned a cigar factory, which he inherited and which had been in existence since 1822. The family Heckscher had lived in Hamburg-Altona since the 16th century, which can be seen from the grave stones on the old, Jewish cemetery in the Koenigstasse in Altona.

I attended the Realschule (high school) at the Holstentor from Eater 1884 to Easter 1894 and passed the 'Einjaehrige Freiwilligen Reife Pruefung' (a kind of matriculation) on 5 March 1894.

My apprenticeship took place in a raw-tobacco firm in Hamburg, as preparation for my entering my father's factory. This took place in 1898. In 1910, I became the sole owner. In the same year, my brother-in-law, Albert Lippstant, owner of a large clothing factory with 300 female workers, became ill (paralysis of the brain) and had to live in a sanatorium till he died in 1918. I was forced to enter this factory so as to make it possible for my sister to maintain her existence. However, I could not permanently lead two large enterprises and had to liquidate the cigar factory in 1915.

On 7 December 1918, I became co-owner and after a few years sole owner of the clothing factory.

Because of the special knowledge I acquired, I became president of the 'Arbeitsgeberverband der Waechenhersteller Hamburgs und Umgenung' (an association of clothing manufacturers) soon after the First World War. I kept this post till the association was dissolved by the Hitler regime.

In 1938, because of Hitler, the factory was liquidated. After I had been arrested on 10 November 1938 and sent to a concentration camp in Sachsenhausen, I was forced to emigrate. I fled to the United States....

He goes on to describe now, being fairly old, it was difficult for him to make a living. The whole summary was apparently for the German government, which was to give him, and did give him, a pension. (Helmut)

I have not found the original or any further translation of this document, although it may be in the Helmut Heckscher files. (Zahara)

Article by Helmut Heckscher: Will I Go To Heaven?

Published in Harvard Institute for Learning in Retirement

When I had just learned to talk, my parents had me say a German prayer at bedtime *"Lieber Gott mach mich fromm dass ich in den Hillel komm."* (Dear God, make me devout so that I will get into heaven.") Of course, I didn't know what this meant, but I loved the rhyme of *"fromm"* and *"komm."*

Now that I do know, I'm not sure that I really, really want to go to heaven. I've looked at many paintings and writings about it, and it seems indeed, to be a very pleasant destination, preferable by a long shot to hell. But all the descriptions are likely to come from folks who have never been there. They could be misleading.

Even assuming, of course, that I would be admitted, I want more detailed information about heaven. Would I have to learn to fly on angel's wings? Would I enjoy the eternal bliss when there was not much else to do? So far, I have received no answer to these questions.

Fortunately, I recently found a way out of my quandary. A Unitarian minister has assured me that you can always recognize fellow Unitarians because, when they die, they will come to a road sign. One points *To Heaven*, the other, *To a Discussion About Heaven*. It is the latter road they will take.

Though I'm not a Unitarian, that's the road that would appeal to me too. Since my eternal life is at stake and eternity is extremely long, I want to play it safe – especially if the sign had the subscript:

Discussion Sponsored by HILR

Perhaps I will meet you there.

Helmut Heckscher's
Memorial Service

Brief Biography of Helmut Heckscher

September 18, 1921 to May 21, 2008

Helmut was born in Hamburg to an upper middle class German Jewish family. His dad, Max Heckscher, owned and managed a pajama factory and his mom Frieda Heckscher (nee Liepziger) helped with the accounting and household management.

Although the family was Jewish, and Helmut had his Bar Mitzvah, they were quite assimilated into the mainstream German culture, attending services only on special occasions, and socializing with Jews and gentiles alike. Helmut was a member of a socialist Zionist youth group, but attended a regular non-Jewish school.

Helmut's friend Bob Guttman still remembers them riding bikes together around Hamburg during the elementary school years. After the Nazi rise to power they had to leave the regular school and attend the Talmud Torah segregated school, where Helmut met teachers he remembered fondly for years to come.

In 1938, after the *Kristalnacth* (night of broken glass) the Nazis came and took Max to a concentration camp. Luckily Helmut had befriended a man in Denmark who pulled some strings and got him into the *Kindertransport,* through which Helmut was evacuated to England.

In one of thousands of miracles during that time, Rosa Hoga, the family's Catholic former housekeeper, living in Milwalkee, found someone to sponsor the family. They got their visas, left Germany and Helmut later joined his parents there.

In the US, Helmut served in the army and in occupied Japan after the war, translating interviews of captured German officers. Upon return to the US he studied at Madison, Berkeley and Harvard, where he met Bridget Tancock. After they married, they moved to Newton where David, Zahara and Rachel grew up. After Bridget died, Helmut balanced his career as a scientist with being a single parent. Following his retirement, he pursued his love of gardening, literature, music, and travel. As late as spring 2008 he was taking classes at the Harvard Institute for Learning in Retirement.

In has later years, Helmut was concerned about dying a good death. He let family know that he didn't want to live if he couldn't walk, read, or take care of himself. It was a blessing that he was able to make his own decision about when he no longer wanted heroic measures to keep him alive. In mid May, after a month in hospital, he told his doctors he wanted to turn off the pace maker that was keeping him alive. Rachel, David, and Zahara were all able to be with him in his last days and he died at home under hospice care, with his three children by his side.

One of the caretakers at Neville place where Helmut lived, commented upon his passing that "A man can live many lives in one life." I found this a good summary of Dad's experience, from refugee and survivor, to soldier, student, teacher, scientist, inventor, husband, father, writer, lover of literature, and in his last years the devoted friend of Hale Champion, grandfather to Pheobe, Cecily, and Max, and beloved companion to Margaret Cain, who will remain a cherished part of the family Helmut leaves behind.

Comments from JoAnne Medalie Melman, Friend of Helmut

At Helmut Heckscher's Memorial, July 20, 2008

Remembering Helmut Heckscher

As I grow older, I have become more focused on the larger narrative of all of our lives. The story of Bridget Tancock of Oxford, England and Helmut Heckscher of Hamburg, Germany is shadowed by the events of World War II. Helmut came into my life through Bridget, a beloved chum and friend, beginning with her arrival in Cambridge, MA to attend graduate school in Human Development at Harvard in 1958. The thread of our relationship begins with Vivian Weil, who introduced me to her college roommate, Posey Margaretten, then a graduate student in Human Development at Harvard. It happened that Posey's older sister, Phyllis visiting in Oxford with her meteologist husband, attended a tea party given by locals for American women. There she met Bridget's mother who mentioned that her daughter was soon to go to Boston to graduate school, resulting in a referral to Posey. Posey brought Bridget to meet me and we immediately found common ground. I had spent a post-college year at LSE in London where Bridget first studied sociology. We knew some of the same leftist Trotskyites there and had many similar interests. Although in different programs and years in grad school, we kept close.

Bridget was a robust, life-affirming woman who, like me, had a left-wing take on culture and society. She was deeply committed to "doing good" as was her mother who was a political activist. I called her "old bean" and we made fun of our mutual cultural traditions while honoring them (she coming from an English dissenter background). Her dissertation on mother-child Barbadian households, I think, was an expression of an important theme in her own life narrative. As she neared the end of her professional training, she began looking seriously for a suitable mate. She met Helmut at a gathering at the English-speaking Union in Boston. I remember her telling me that she met a "funny little man" there (she was a big girl) and she was charmed, and the match proceeded.

I do not know the details of Helmut's early narrative in Hamburg, Germany except that he once mentioned to me that as an adolescent, he was in the left-zionist movement. It was only after Joan and Rachel travelled with him to Hamburg for a post-Holocaust rapprochement visit that I learned that he was rescued from Germany on the *Kindertransport* to England. It was there, I assume, that his Anglophilia developed toward the rescuers from his traumatic flight from Germany. Helmut was what used to be called 'a bachelor' pushing 40, Bridget was in her early 30's when they got together and were ready to begin a new family-oriented phase of life (much to my benefit because as David soon came along, I inherited their first apartment in a lovely old house on Appleton Street) and they moved to a house in Belmont near the Weils.

Helmut, the rescue, was a survivor whose governing *modus operandi* remained throughout his life to get what he needed to survive. He was good at finding the resources that would provide a viable life for himself but without much to spare for others. Bridget, on the other hand, was a rescuer if there ever was one, a daughter of a strong mother and a father whose trope was that he lived precariously with a bullet wound from the war and needed care-taking. In this respect, she came from a mother-child household and was prepared to be the principal care-taker and life-giver of the emerging family. This was an ideal match for Helmut until tragedy struck with Bridget's cancer. There is an old Hasidic saying: "Man plans, God Laughs." Helmut was overwhelmed by his loss and new responsibilities of parenthood.

His survival instincts prevailed however. Helmut was able to call on and use the support of friends in this crisis and another rescuer emerged, Marion Sanders, for whom I am a link in the narrative thread. We became friends in graduate school and I linked Marion to Bridget. By the time Rachel was born, I had left for New York and while there were family visits to New York and the Cape before, during and after Bridget's death, with Helmut's support, Marion became a steady presence and advisor (with a little consultation on the side from me). Thus, while he could not be a rescuer for David, Joan and Rachel, he did provide a model for using the available resources that contributed to their becoming the resourceful, competent, caring adults that they are now. As he declined in recent years, with the vicissitudes of aging, I am sure he was gratified by their successful lives and their caring concern. At the end of his journey he can rest in peace.

Comments from Marguerite Rosenthal, Friend of Helmut

At Helmut Heckscher's Memorial, July 2008

For Helmut Heckscher

I am truly sorry that I cannot be with Helmut's family and friends on this day as you remember and celebrate his life. As I write this, I am in Vermont - where Helmut and Margaret visited me a number of years ago – and awaiting my grandson's arrival from Washington. I must get him to the airport for a noon return flight from Burlington on the 20th. Thus, joining you for this important occasion is impossible for me. Instead, I hope my few words here will convey both the sorrow I feel on his passing and my admiration and caring for the man he was.

Helmut was, I'm quite certain, the first friend (outside of work companions) that I made when I moved to Boston 21 years ago. And where did we meet? At a singles event in West Newton that was held in the Second Church, mid-week (as far as I know, it ceased functioning years ago). The subject that night was El Salvador and, specifically, the murder of the priest, Oscar Romero; obviously, this wasn't a typical singles event and perhaps that is why both Helmut and I were in attendance.

What grew from that meeting was an important friendship that included chats, movies, walks, political conversations, the occasional concert and – until he met Margaret – the sharing of confidences, hopes, and disappointments.

Helmut's life reflected so much of the 20th century's worst and best: Nazi Germany and the almost magical story of his family's move to the US through the compassion of their housekeeper (if I'm remembering correctly); his military service and post-war education that resulted in a career in science; marriage and 3 children - and ultimately the death of his wife and the resulting responsibility for those children. How wonderful that Helmut lived long enough to see his children happily married and to become a grandfather of 3. Lucky, too, that he did meet Margaret and that they had such a mutually supportive, interesting, and enjoyable several years together.

When I think about Helmut's outstanding characteristic, what comes clearest to mind are his intellectual curiosity and a willingness to take on challenges and venture into new territory. His volunteer work and the

Museum of Science (this is what he was doing when I first knew him), his long association with the HILR – where he both took and gave courses – (I'm sorry I didn't take his course on utopias—at least I think it was his course), his participation in his books, his delving into and writing about his genealogy, his interest in contemporary political problems, and even his skepticism about evolution were all reflections of a person with an appetite for discovery. And quirks: oil but never vinegar on salad, for instance. Vacations often mirrored taste for the unusual (the boat trip on the Amazon, for instance), and he was an adventurer. I am thinking now of the long bike ride he suggested that we took on Martha's Vineyard, headed from Vineyard Haven to my friend's house in Gay Head (when was that? Eighteen or so years ago?); this adventure resulted in Helmut's being hospitalized with a mild heart attack (sorry to bring up the not so pleasant memory). He remained, however, intrepid, optimistic and in good health.

I regret, of course, that I was somewhat out of touch with Helmut over the last couple of years and was unaware of his last illness. I did not get to say goodbye, but I will surely remember Helmut with great respect and affection, always.

Comments from Margaret Cain,
Helmut's Partner and Companion

At Helmut Heckscher's Memorial, July 2008

Appreciating Helmut

I met Helmut at the UU Book Group in 1996. My first impression was that he was a little weird; he brought book reviews but apparently hadn't really read the book. That summer, he invited me to a book talk, our first date, and I began to appreciate both his appreciation of books and his quirks as a part of his charm.

And Helmut was charming: his soft voice, his European accent, his laugh, and the way his eyes could light up. His courtship overcame my reluctance to get involved. That reluctance came from having been widowed – but he shared that – and the age difference – would I lose him soon? Well, we started "going steady" and had almost twelve years of good companionship.

In reviewing those years, I find I focus on the many things we did together, his special characteristics, and Helmut as a fine model for the later part of life.

Starting with that first book talk, we had heard many lectures: Helmut always listened carefully so that he could as a good question at the end. These ranged from Observatory Night at the Harvard-Smithsonian Center for Astrophysics through natural history talks and book talks to pre-performance lectures at the opera. Mostly at my initiative, we attended many concerts and Helmut managed to stay awake though most of them. At the end of most plays, Helmut would say, "I really didn't understand it at all" and then proceed to discuss various scenes.

We traveled many places quite well together, soaking up news scenes and information. I need to admit that, Helmut added some special travel challenges for me. First was airport security, which only got more complicated during that time. Helmut had a pacemaker and later a defibrillator so that he always needed a personal inspection. Add to that the huge collection of things he always had in his pockets, especially the interval timer that I had given him to time his naps (it could beep unaccountably). We definitely needed to allow plenty of time to clear security. The other memorable challenge was laundry. Helmut usually packed light with just a few changes of clothes but always a radio and plenty of reading material. However, his essential tremor tended to provide plenty of spilled coffee and that left stains on the white shirts he favored. So, often our room would be draped with drying laundry. On the ship in Norway, Helmut stayed in the cabin in his pj's when he ran out of clean clothes, while I tackled the Norwegian-style laundromat.

I could spend lots of time on travels but suggest that we discuss these informally. I've brought along two photo albums from trips. Here's a partial list: St. John in the US Virgin Islands in a rented villa, Cold River AMC camp, most of New England including several Cape Cod vacations, D.C., Costa Rica twice - rain and sun, London, his hometown of Hamburg, France via auto and barge, Florida, Arizona (it was really cold both times), Norway, Panama (yes, through the canal), Ireland with driver-guide Kevin Leahy, Galapagos where Helmut LOVED the baby sea lions, Hawaii to visit Rachel and Eric, and Sicily, inspired by readings in our HILR class on the literature of travel. Because Helmut's walking was slowing down during these years, he was good at suggesting that we focus on a few key items to see each day. Slowing and savoring has advantages.

Helmut has provided a fine model for living one's later years.

First of all, he was interested in all sorts of information: great literature, news of the day, scientific advances and controversies, biographies... He couldn't resist picking up any available printed matter and discarded it with difficulty. Many trees have been sacrificed for printouts of information he found on the Internet. Probably many of us here have received articles from Helmut and wondered whether we should be appreciative or slightly insulted. He also really enjoyed radio interviews and programs in which listeners call in for discussion. He LOVED the Harvard Institution for Learning in Retirement (HILR), almost always taking the maximum number of courses. At Neville Place, discussions with Hale Champion were rewarding for both men. I agreed with Hale that Helmut would take a strong contrarian view just to prolong a discussion.

Next, he kept in motion. When we went to Cold River Camp he did sometimes hike, yearning for a bathtub and ice cream on the down portion of one. Later, he stopped driving. Then, he really learned how to use public transportation to get all over the greater Boston (e.g., three buses to Newtonville). He walked too – slower and slower – for pleasure along Fresh Pond or trudging through Harvard Square with a loaded briefcase.

Furthermore, he tackled several major projects (in addition to little inventions involving wires and solder). One was the Heckscher genealogy. Another was the Pintus inheritance. The one left incomplete was his own autobiography. On this, he worked very hard, not only on organizing the information but also in trying to make it an interesting reading. On this and in general, he was concerned about using the right word and pronouncing it properly.

Finally, he dealt conscientiously with health issues and medical matters. (He described himself as a good hypochondriac.) Although his concerns were sometimes misplaced, he did use medical systems assertively and effectively and sought out both information and treatments. Checking on side effects, researching new treatments, and making suggestions to his collection of doctors, seems to me the very model of a modern older gentleman (almost Gilbert and Sullivan).

I will treasure these lessons.

I will hold these wonderful memories.

Biography of Bridget by Catherine "Kitty" Wise Spence Tancock nee Adams, Mother of Bridget

Catherine Bridget Heckscher (nee Tancock)

1ˢᵗ Nov 1928 - 8ᵗʰ Sept 1976

Bridget was born in Reading, but only because there was a good maternity home there (more suitable than a boys' school house), but soon came home to her real home at Wellesley House at Wellington College, of which her Father was housemaster. He had only been promoted to this job that term, having been in-college tutor to the Combermere dormitory for 10 years, living in bachelor quarters till 1927, when we were married and went into a flat built for us as an addition to the dormitory. After one academic year there, we had to move to the big house with forty boys and a domestic staff of nine, plus gardener and gardener's boy, and that was where Bridget's early life was spent (1928-1941). It was my duty to help Osborne in his job of house master by managing the domestic side – catering for meals, engaging staff and a hundred other jobs – all new to me. Motherhood was new too, so I had engaged an experienced nurse temporarily to see me through my baby's first month or so and "show me the ropes." But I soon saw that if she was to be properly looked after and lead a regular life I must keep Nannie on – if I tried to look after Bridget myself entirely, I'd have been constantly interrupted and she would suffer. This is one of the penalties of an institutional life such as we led – for example,

Osborne and I had breakfast and lunch in the dining hall daily with the boys so the little girls had theirs in their nursery with Nannie.

Bridget was a fine baby and always very healthy. I breastfed her until she was about 7 or 8 months old and then (in the midst of weaning her) I had to leave her to Nannie and bottles and dash up to Scotland where my mother had suddenly died (she had stayed with us at the time of Bridget's birth and was to have come again in August 1929, but died after an emergency operation). So Bridget never knew her.

Wellesley House had a large beautiful garden with a huge lawn just behind the house and a grass tennis court beyond that - a huge copper beech tree on one side and on the other a big lime tree under which Bridget lay in her pram and slept or watched the leaves blowing. We had an old gardener, who also looked after the pigs and hens (fed partly on kitchen waste etc.). He was full of old sayings and quaint talk and interested in the children; and Bridget was given a lovely little wheelbarrow by her godfather, and spent many happy hours in the garden and wandering with me in the bit of open country with heather and birch trees just opposite our front door.

Elizabeth Wright, an early playmate and daughter of a colleague of Osborne's, wrote me recently, "We were so lucky to have our childhood at Wellington and I remember endless sunny days when we wandered free - It seems that we wandered for miles but I expect it was only a few hundred yards from home - and we were always happy and never cross or bored!"

I was very happy in those pre-Hitler days. I can remember very clearly just after I got home with my new baby saying to myself, "How happy I am! What have I ever done to deserve such happiness?" with this fine baby and the joy of working with my husband and his beloved boys and living in such a lovely place.

We did work hard and had lots of problems of course, and we felt we had to escape into the holidays by ourselves for a bit from institutional life, so when the children were young, we only took them on visits to Osborne's old home in Essex, where his father lived with his daughters, Alice and Nina, (he died in 1930) or to Torquay where my sister, Mary, kept a house for an uncle.

Bridget's sister Mary was born in 1931, Ruth in 1934.

To return to Bridget, I was able to teach her myself at first (she could read when she was four), and we had lovely walks and talks in those woods and plenty of fun. She was a big girl and had long golden plaits, blue eyes, and pink cheeks. I quote Elizabeth Wright again, "I can see her as if it were yesterday – always rather mature and a calming influence. Her great thick plaits were always a source of enormous envy to me."

I think she was a responsible and rather serious child and when Mary and Ruth were born, she was at first protective and always the "big sister..."

I started taking her once a week to "singing games" at Ravenswood – a small private school with a fair number of local "Kindergarten" children and some older boarders whose parents were abroad. Singing games were usually nursery rhymes and songs and round games needing a number of children. The next year she began "going to school" daily at Ravenswood.

I didn't think the standard of learning was very high, but she seemed quite happy there and Mrs. Aspinall was a kind motherly person with one or two young assistants.

When Bridget was old enough, she started at The Holt (county secondary school for girls) at Wokingham, about four miles away, to which she went by bus or bike with several other local girls, including Elizabeth Wright and Shelia Stocken (daughter of another colleague). This must have been about 1938 (I think?) when the menace of Hitler was in the background of our lives. Then in December came the Polio epidemic in College during which twenty boys developed the disease and one died. Most parents took their boys home at the outset of the epidemic but some developed it there. By February, it was considered safe to re-open the school and life returned to normal. We had no cases in the Wellesley – perhaps because we were some distance from the main buildings, perhaps because our boys fed in the house and all their meals were cooked there. The cause of the outbreak was never clearly established, though it was thought likely that there might be a carrier among those of the kitchen staff who lived in the village and came in daily to the central kitchen.

Like everyone else, Osborne and I had plenty on our minds when the summer term came to an end in 1939. However, we did have a family holiday at Seascale on the coast of Westmoreland, only a few miles from Wasdale in the Lake District. There we met my only two sisters, May and Meta, who also had taken rooms in the village, and had their car with them. This meant that those who wanted could go by car to the lakes and mountains inland and walk and climb, while others could stay by the sea and bathe etc. Weather was fine and we all enjoyed ourselves.

But the news was bad, and war seemed impending, so we were driven to home before our time was up.

It had been planned that I should take the children to Scotland and deposit them at my aunt and uncle's "safe" home at Lochgoilhead, Argyll, and then follow Osborne, who was to go straight home and start on arranging for wartime life, blacking-out, etc.

The night before we left, I could not sleep and in the morning, I said to Osborne, "I just can't do this. Let's take them all home with us." And we did. We wired Nannie who was on holiday, and took the train South. She was on the doorstep to receive us, and when the three saw her they all shouted "Nannie." And I said to myself, "I can't send her away now" (as I earlier planned to do). So she stayed with us till we left the Wellesley, though by that time Ruth was seven. I still think we did right to keep her on.

Wartime changed school life greatly and made it busier than ever. During the air raids the boys went to the shelter that had been built for them underground and we (family and domestic staff) to the cellar. Wellington was expected to be a popular target for raids, as the building was conspicuous and only about three miles from Sandhurst and the Staff College and not very much more from Aldershot. But nothing worth recording happened until in October 1940 two bombs were dropped on Wellington and the Master was killed. All boys were safe underground and he was the only casualty, having opened his front door to see what was happening just as the whole porch was smashed by blast. He was a young man and bachelor and had only been Master since 1937. Naturally, this was a great shock to the whole community. The Second Master took over as acting head until a successor was appointed in 1941.

Meanwhile, Osborne's time as housemaster came to an end in the spring of 1941 (as he was 55). Numbers throughout the school had fallen and it was decided to close the house (on his retiral) and distribute our boys to different houses and dormitories, while the Wellesley building was let for the duration to the preparatory school of St. Paul's (London) the senior part of which was already housed in the district sharing our playing fields, swimming bath [illegible] in Crowthorne.

We moved into a smaller house (Rosset), which we rented from the College to whom it belonged, though it was a short way outside the grounds, and we stayed there till Osborne's final retirement at sixty (1946) when we came to Oxford. Nannie had left us in 1941, and we lived an ordinary family with the three girls at school. Mary went to the Holt in, I think, in September 1941 and Ruth followed in 1944. They had to live the austere life of wartime with food rationing and clothes rationing, blackouts etc. and I of course cooked and (after a short time with one of our Wellesley maids) had only a little sporadic domestic help. I got involved in various voluntary organisations, I ran a fruit preservation centre for the Women's

Institute (making supplies of Jam for the local shops and canning fruit from our own gardens) and so forth. Osborne was in the College Home Guard and taught the R.A.F. section of the Officer's Training Corps Meteorology and Astronomy ("Met. and Astro.").

We now sent Bridget to boarding school, as the local secondary school hadn't good enough facilities for senior work. She went to St. Swithun's School, Winchester, and was there for two school years only. The school buildings had been commandeered as a military hospital before she went there and the girls were evacuated to a number of houses on the outskirts of Winchester – less convenient of course. The school still wore uniform, and this was a problem, as it took a good many "clothing coupons" to fit out a big girl like Bridget, and she was at a disadvantage as compared with those who had come earlier and collected clothes over two or three years. There were things she had to do without.

We gave up our car pretty soon after leaving the Wellesley and in any case petrol was scarce. But the train journey to Winchester was not too bad for war-time and she came home at half-term and the holidays and I visited her at school for special occasions, about once a term, and Osborne's cousin and her husband lived in Winchester and asked her out and also put me up several times, so that I had a day or two with her.

It was at St. Swithun's that Bridget learnt the excellent habit of writing home regularly – once a week usually – and I have got some of her letters, though I have destroyed many. They are full of enthusiasm about school doings and I think she learnt a great deal and became self-reliant and able to cope.

But she also gives the impression of longing to get home for the holidays and be with her family and friends. The chief friend she made at St. Swithun's was Bess Finlayson, whom you know now in Boston. One or two other girls came to stay with us in the holidays as well as Bess but they not seem to have kept in touch with Bridget for long after leaving school.

In 1946, Bridget left school and came home in time to help with our move to Oxford; for Osborne had reached the retiring age (60). He had a certain amount of illness and seemed glad to give up, though I am sure he missed his boys and his teaching. We managed to buy a rather inconvenient Victorian house in St. Margaret's Road and sent Mary and Ruth to the Oxford High School for Girls. Bridget found it hard to decide what to do next. The year before, when the Oxford and Cambridge women's college circularised girls' schools asking them not to send any but "outstanding" girls to them, as they already had a backlog from war-time waiting to come up, Bridget firmly decided that she was not "outstanding" and would not attempt to take the entrance exam, but do the Higher Certificate which would qualify her for some other University (as a matter of she was as "outstanding" as many others who were successful).

I suggested that she might take a social science diploma at the London School of Economics and become a hospital almoner. She agreed to try this. But when we went to make arrangements at L.S.E. (newly returned from war-time evacuation to Bristol and still in a confused state), we were told that she could not start on this course until she was a year older. She would be allowed to enter for a Sociology degree if she took two more subjects in Higher Certificate. So she worked for these at home, and having qualified, began her degree course in October 1947. The present scheme of grants had not begun then and we were rather "hard up," so she was always a poor student and lived as cheaply as she could in various places – for a while in a hotel but mostly in bed-sitters or sharing with another girl. In vacations she usually found some temporary job and ultimately was given a small allowance by some fund in Oxford. Her last year (1949-50) she and her friend Ursula Mackintosh both lived at Nutford House, a London University hostel when Bridget was working very hard for her finals and Ursula was also at L.S.E. Ursula is the daughter of my lifelong friend, and these two girls used to come together to Oxford for weekends. In 1948, Ursula, Bridget and Mary when to the Lake and had a wonderful youth hostelling 10-14 days, walking for miles and climbing in beautiful hot weather, and hitched back visiting York on their way to London. Mary was in her last year at school.

In August 1951, Bridget and Ursula had a week's holiday in Paris, exploring and thrilling over the Louvre and various galleries, etc. By this time Ursula had a personnel-managing job with a big firm in Birmingham and Bridget had gone to a town-planning post in Leicester.

At that time, Town Planning (including developing new town and housing estates) was a rather new thing in England and though Bridget could see that a sociologist's ideas about the life and needs of future dwellers therein should be considered, the planner preferred to use only architects and people with qualifications connected with building and land etc. So she realised that she had better try another line, left Leicester and returned to London. Finally she decided on work connected with education and felt that for this she must have practical teaching experience. So she spent a year at the London Institute of Education training as a secondary school teacher, and then took a very tough job at a London Secondary Modern school.

Reflections on the Life
of Bridget Heckscher,
1976, MIT Chapel

These are the collected statements from friends of Bridget Heckscher, nee Catherine Bridget Tancock, at her Memorial Service. Bridget (1931-1976) was born in Reading, England. She attended the London School of Economics and then came to the US to pursue her EdD at Harvard. That is where she met Helmut Heckscher, who she married in about 1959. She was the mother of David, Joan (now Zahara) and Rachel.

Comments from Posey Rogolsky, Friend of Bridget

At Bridget Heckscher's Memorial, 1976

Just eighteen years ago Bridget burst into my apartment without warning, fresh from the plane. She was just entering Harvard, frightened by the eminent reputation of the University and reassured that Saul, to whom I had just been engaged, was also going to be in the same department. The bustle of our engagement allowed us only brief encounters but I knew that Bridget was a rare spirit, a soul mate, and I admired her courage about making a new life. Her wit delighted me and soon it was possible to penetrate the English reserve and find the clear, often-amused perceptions beneath.

We became strong telephone friends. She was not used to the frank comments on others that "the ladies" (Joanne, Vivian and me) would use, but never missed a nuance and had her own delicate signal system for indicating negative opinions. Bridget was wonderfully tactful and careful but when her voice took on a vague and distracted tone, I would be alerted to her perception of something amiss.

During [those] student years when Bridget was single, she would often toss bouquets in my lap that made me uncomfortable, her admiration of my family, my career, etc. It was probably her way of saying that she wasn't sure that she would ever make it in achieving her goals, but she seemed so industrious, and free of neurotic stumbling blocks that I knew she was clearly heading in a forward direction. I suppose Bridget was really insecure about achievement and may have felt overpowered by the verbally brilliant friends we shared, but I was never able to really believe her insecurity because she seemed so able.

When Bridget married, we, her friends, were delighted. I remember the joyous quality of the wedding reception. We loved to compare husbands who shared some noble and petty qualities. I think we both knew that we were fortunate in having truly caring and dependable men, but we both laughed about Saul's $5 suits and Helmut's mail-order shoes.

I think I was especially pleased that Bridget married a Jew, albeit a non-observant one, because it strengthened the sisterly tie we had felt. Her full acceptance of the Jewishness of her friends was a special pleasure to us; she really seemed to rise above ancient prejudices. On the other hand, knowing Bridget has reinforced my impression of the English and increased my admiration for them. Her ability to cope, to make a full and enriching life in the span of eighteen years, seems to be an especially English trait.

It has been ten years since we left Boston and we have seen little of the Heckschers. Of course, we always thought that meeting with good friends could be postponed because it was always so easy to pick up the threads of friendship. I remember the ebullient, half-feigning, drunk Bridget of Alex' Bar Mitzvah and enclose a picture to document that great moment.

When Bridget became sick in the fall, mortality and death suddenly came home to us. I knew as she surely knew, that her time was very limited. Her spunkiness and determination to give every bit of herself to the children and to Helmut may have determined her remission as much as the doctors. Rather than collapsing into depression, she seemed intent on making the best of every moment she had left to live. Her health was so convincing when we visited in June, that we could have a merry time. The children seemed remarkable, sturdy, gentle and sweet and her dealings with them was wonderful to see, especially since I had not seen her in a mother's role very much. It was so reassuring to see her that, even though we knew her health could not last indefinitely, she seemed to have pushed back the disease into a bad memory.

If one has to die, it is best to die Bridget's way, without prolonged suffering and with all your senses intact. Nevertheless, her death meant a great and sudden loss to us all. I come from a very big family and at that time, when Helmut was able to turn to us for advice and comfort, it came home to me that we, Bridget's friends <u>were</u> her family.

Visiting with Helmut and the children last weekend was enormously meaningful to me. The love in the family and among her friends seemed to be a reflection of the strong ties which Bridget had made. I had never really talked to Helmut until that weekend but he made it possible for use to share his grief and to feel close to him. I never was so struck with goodness showing itself in a person as I was with Helmut in his wrestling with his loss and sorrow, his will to be true to the memory of Bridget and to be responsible in every way. I think all of us were overcome with admiration, and in my case, it was for someone I had hardly known before this sad time.

The memorial service was done with dignity and grace, and the sense of union among us all was palatable. Again, like the minister, the remarkable offerings of Bridget's' friends touched me and made me proud to be a member of such a circle. Somehow my priorities got reordered and I realized that friendship, decency, and good human ties had been waylaid by conventional pursuits. I resolved to do better. It was our good fortune to know her; our sadness to lose such a good friend and person.

Comments from Vivian Weil, Friend of Bridget

At Bridget Heckscher's Memorial, 1976

I don't know who was the first of us to meet Bridget – JoAnne, Posey, or Marion. It wasn't me because I was the only one of us not in school, and Bridget had come as a Fulbright scholar to Harvard. Looking back, I think we all realized immediately what a person had landed in our midst.

In the early days I knew her as clever, curious, and observant, interested in America, and in us, me and my family. Soon she became interwoven in the life of our family - spending immobilized blizzard days in the snow with her children, bringing mince pies at Christmas, and using us for subjects in her research. I remember a particularly searching survey into my goals in child-rearing which I always thought in some curious way strengthened the bond between us.

In those first eight years of Bridget's time here, I think that most, if not all, our important occasions were shared. Finishing the dissertation, the first job at Wheelock, the wedding ceremony with the Chinese Justice of the Peace – by hilarious report – the champagne reception, and buying the house on Goden Street. Sometime in this period, Bridget began writing the occasional poems which she presented for our trips abroad, movings, and other large undertakings.

It was a fabric of life we made together. We were all self-conscious, self-critical, and objects of scrutiny to one another. Bridget contributed a note of irony, especially self-irony, as I came to appreciate. Until her children arrived, I enjoyed and profited from Bridget's particular talents for living without explicitly realizing what they were. As I watched her manage teaching and babies and friends and au pair girls, I began to observe her capacity for recognizing the tasks at hand and their priorities and for coping with them smoothly in their turn.

In 1966 was the great exodus when most of us moved away, but Bridget and Helmut had bought the big house in Newton. I found that house very satisfying, knowing that Bridget could make an English home and have a base for us to come back to in Boston.

In fact, there were not many reunions, but the threads held. I was pleased to observe at a distance over and over again in Bridget's comments on politics, sociology, the women's movement, that she was tuned in to what was really going on, and she helped to expose it. Her instinct for reality was general, not limited to her immediate projects. When we did meet and I experienced the ease of her family life, I would recall her remarkable ability to carry on.

I didn't truly come to appreciate what had always been Bridget's attachment to life and her hold on living until her illness. Somehow this period has etched for me her remarkable awareness, self-consciousness, irony and command of the concrete details of ongoing life. She seemed to me to deal with her illness with those qualities especially. She was so successful in her reassertion of ongoing life that it was shattering to learn four of five weeks ago that she hadn't prevailed. I am comforted to know that what she faced until the end was life. I mourn the loss of Bridget.

Comments from JoAnne Medalie Melman, Friend of Bridget

At Bridget Heckscher's Memorial, 1976

Reflections on the Life of my Friend, Bridget Tancock Heckscher

I speak today not only out of a need to bear witness to a life that touched me profoundly and to share love, admiration and respect I feel for Bridget but as a familial duty to an adopted sister. I know Bridget would have expected no less, though with her characteristic tact, she would not have asked it of me directly.

She blew into town from London, just 18 years ago, in early September 1958 (Posey and Saul recently reminded me), finding our circle though a chance meeting in Oxford between her mother and Posey's older sister. I remember her as a sturdy, robust apple-cheeked young Englishwoman, eager for new experiences and full of enthusiasm for what she regarded as the liberated spirit of modernity she found in the new world. We were all then in our late twenties, and for several of us, our permanent life commitments to career and mates were still in flux. In the throes of becoming 'my own woman' as they say today, Bridget impressed me especially then with her venturesome spirit in leaving homeland and family for a new and unpredictable life course. That first year we met only a few times in Cambridge. She was taken up with her new graduate studies, and I with activities that led to my decision to enter graduate school in September 1959.

It was as fellow graduate students in Human Development at Harvard that our friendship flourished. Through those stimulating and stressful years as graduate students we offered each other camaraderie, support, and mutual reinforcement for our ambivalent, self-doubting, amused sense of ourselves as emerging professional women. I was reminded of how much her work was a part of Bridget's identity at our last visit just one week before she died. Though she was struggling then with acute discomfort and fear for her deteriorating body, she asked me about a paper I had written (still performing as a social facilitator despite her dire situation). The she reminded me of the paper she had hoped to write for an upcoming conference, with the comment "I don't think I'm going to make it." Tragically, I could not disagree with her for I knew she was trying to help me to confront the fact that her hold on this life was slipping fast.

It was her hold on life, her sense of reality, her readiness to embrace the possible and to cope with life's opportunities, tasks and burdens, that uniquely characterize Bridget for me. She was a doer -- a competent, activist who, unlike me, did not waste time on obsessional perfectionistic aspirations. I watched with awe as she tackled her dissertation research and writing so forthrightly and competently and, when that was within sight of completion, she managed to give off the signals that drew Helmut to her to complete the next developmental task she has set for herself. As we old friends often commented to each other, Bridget was the embodiment of what used to be called 'character.' Character, not in the dutiful, dreary sense of the overburdened super-ego (though she had that too sometimes), but in her good sense about what was important and her steadfastness in her multiple roles as friend, colleague, wife and mother. I used to call her 'old bean' which to me conveyed the English character trait she wore so lightly and always with a sense of mirth and irony.

I have been musing in the last week on what led our relationship to endure over the years beyond the situational factors that originally drew us together. She was the thoroughgoing sociologist by character and personality, committed to a belief in the primacy of rationality and the possibility of achieving conscious control over her destiny. I, on the other hand, the Jewish intellectual out of small town America, was at that time much more the interior person deeply immersed in the mysteries of psychoanalysis and impressed with the power of the irrational and uncontrollable. By ideology, I was not even a muted feminist as Bridget was in those days, spurred on by her Scottish nonconformist mother who has been a crusader in many a good fight. Bridget was both fascinated and amused by my own and our mutual friends' preoccupation with the psychological interiors of lives. Her inimitable poems for all occasions often reflected her skepticism and gave us all a good laugh. I wish I had one now to read.

What we shared was a sense of social marginality, coupled with a need to belong to a social structure that we selected rather than had imposed upon us by the past. She was an Englishwoman in America, not totally at one with either culture, a pragmatic, achievement oriented woman who had rejected the most conventional routes on the life cycle. We shared, too, a common quest to gain control over pasts yet a feeling for tradition and even ritual which got expressed in the extended family we helped form. I think now that our differences in emphasis and personal style may actually have permitted our relatively unambivalent sisterly bond to emerge. Both oldest sisters in actuality, we were able to at least partially free ourselves from the competitive strains we had experiences in our families of origin. And the differences in orientation lessened as we both faced the vicissitudes of middle adulthood. Bridget became more comfortable with the irrational and emotional life. I became more connected with life's reality, constraints and demands, and impressed with the competent, steady hand that held and nurtured those splendid infants and resourceful, zestful, uncommonly competent children. In recent years, we both warmed to the new feminist consciousness and added this perspective to our periodic summings up when we met. Yet these feminist leanings were not in conflict with her traditional homey values. Her remarkable life achievement was that she was able to integrate her enduring concern and talent for parenthood with her work by finally evolving a career in which she could foster the art of parenting in others.

Out of a long line of octogenarians whom she mentioned and kept in touch with, I always thought of Bridget as the sturdiest and most indestructible of all. It is a cruel irony that Bridget who above all embodied the reality principle to us should be the one to force us to confront death. As in all else in her life as I saw it, she sought the possible when she knew she was stricken, but she accepted the inevitable when there was no other choice. I am grateful that with her usual foresight she saw to it that we would say goodbye to each other that last week. I feel a piece of my life has gone with her, but Bridget has left me with a deepened sense of what it is to be a real human being.

Comments from Miles F. Shore, MD, Co-worker of Bridget

At Bridget Heckscher's Memorial, 1976

Bridget Heckscher worked at the Massachusetts Mental Health Center for a little more than four years. Although she was already an experienced educator who had taught at Wheelock and Emmanuel Colleges and at Boston University, she began in the mental health systems as a neophyte, writing grants, helping with the details of launching new programs in order to learn what the peculiar world of mental health is all about.

Over the four years she was asked to take on more and more responsibility and at the last, as a director of our community child program, she was one of the people we counted on most. She had major administrative responsibilities, for she had to oversee nearly a dozen constituent programs spread throughout our catchment area. But along the way she had also been a very strong person, developing and leading educational groups for parents and supervising work in our home daycare programs.

Of course, her professional success was based on her competence and seriousness of purpose. But it was also due to the fact that she managed to capture the hearts of everyone who worked with her, whatever their race or sex or circumstances of life. That was no mean feat for a white woman from the suburbs with a doctor's degree from Harvard and a British accent!

People remembered how much she cared about children -- how important it was to her that they have a chance to grow in every way. And they remembered how sure she was that education would help in that growth. She was a real teacher, absolutely convinced that education was irresistible. She herself couldn't resist being a student and would turn up at lectures and seminars at our place to keep up her own learning. She was simply incredulous that our trainees would not attend everything that was offered.

Her conviction about children's needs led her into the most effective kind of advocacy. She made it work not only because she was so convinced and gently persistent, but more because she kept herself out of it. She was an advocate, not because she enjoyed finding fault or had a personal axe to grind, but simply because children had great needs. Her advocacy most often took the form of helping people to do the job they were supposed to do. She spent endless hours in the last six months writing letters, calling and visiting foundations to scrape up money for the programs under her wing. Most often, they were small amounts for a field trip or some play equipment -- those little extras which are so important because they are often harder to come by than large grants.

Her capacity to talk comfortably with anyone was almost legendary. It was based in large part on her own directness and lack of pretense. Dorothy Emory, one of our black workers, told me about Bridget's introduction to black eyed peas at Dorothy's house. Just at the moment Bridget arrived for lunch all the chairs were taken so Bridget plopped down on the floor. Dorothy's remonstrance and hustle to find her own chair were countered by Bridget's very firm, "oh posh," and she stayed where she was.

She was so empty and easy to deal with, but she was also tough. It was her misfortune to agree to serve as director of our community child grant just before a terrible fiscal/administrative crisis. It occupied all of us for several months and Bridget took a major part of the heat though it was in no way her fault. She handled it with intelligence and great strength and when it was over managed to put the operation on a much firmer footing than ever before.

I suppose that the most poignant recollection for all of us is the way she carried herself during her illness. She knew very well from the beginning that it was a serious matter. Yet she kept steadily at her life with all the energy and interest that she could muster. As Alice McLerran put it, "she refused to live out of a suitcase," and she did it with such dignity and good humor. As far as I could tell there was never a hint of denial of the reality, no self-pity and a remarkable disinclination to burden other people with her tragedy. If anything she was a little apologetic about being so sick as if she disliked bothering us with it. Most of all, I think she hated to have it interfere with getting the job done. During her last talk with Millie Zanditon she was most concerned with our finding a good replacement for her to get on with the work.

Bridget was a rare person; talented, steady in her purposes and with a simple dignity which touched everyone who knew her. What do we do with her loss? Perhaps the best is to be grateful for what she gave to us in spirit and strength.

Our echoes roll from soul to soul
and grow forever and forever

- Tennyson

End Notes

1   I remember Helmut telling me that the letter "X" was not used very much in German, so "Hoexter," also spelled "Höxter," might have seemed like an unusual and hard to pronounce word, and changed to "Heckscher," which was a word known to the Jewish community. A "heckscher" (more often spelled "hechsher"), is the certification that a rabbi confers upon a food to certify that it is kosher – in modern times, in the US, usually a letter in a circle printed on a food label. I am not sure how Helmut knew these Jews spoke Yiddish or how that relates to the name. I found the following information in the Helmut Heckscher files (Zahara): "Der Hame Heckscher stammt vn den Orte Hoxter in (word unclear). Im Hohelbuch des Sanwil Heckscher Nr. 108 ist eine Beschneidung des Jacob, Sohn des Weir, im Dorfe Otterbergen, werbessert "im Dorfe Bruchhausen" neben Heckscher vergeiennet. Hun liegen diese beidon Dorfer neben der grosseren Stadt Hoxter. Dass Heckscher oine Ortsbegeiohung ist, gent auch aus Nr. 3 des Mohelbuches hervor, in welchem ein Matias in Heckscher und in Nr. 6 sein Neffe Arjai (word unclear), Sohn seines Bruders in Heckscher erwahnt ist. Wahrscheinlich wurde Hoxter hebraisch Heckscher genannt. In den Akten des Archivs der Stadt Altona warden ja auch die Sohne des Ruben Heckscher bur Hoxter genannt." Source: Die folgende Abhandlung stammt von dem Leo Baeck Institute, 129 East 73rd street, New York, N.Y.

2   In 2016, I corresponded with Professor Claudia Schnurmann, who is an expert in the history of German Jews in the Hamburg area, to verify the details. It appears that Helmut made some small errors in his original text, which said: "The name Heckscher first appeared in the late 1500's in a Jewish shtetl near the small town of Hoexter in Eastern Germany." Professor Schnurmann wrote to me that "It [the

Jewish part of Hoexter] was not a shtetl in the Russian or Polish style but only one small alley, the so-called "Judengasse" within the small town Höxter not in eastern Germany but in the western territories of the Holy German Empire. The small but rather beautiful town belonged to the territory of Corvey. He was Catholic while the town turned in 1533 to Protestantism. Within the town was a group of 20 to 40 Jewish families whose ancestors many centuries before might have come from Palestine to Europe . . . Hamburg is situated north of Höxter . . . Ephraim Maier probably was born in 1580."

3   Various versions of the genealogy are in a red binder in the Helmut Heckscher files. (Zahara)

4   An interesting article about this branch of the family is "Charles August Heckscher: A Model Self-Made Man and Merchant in the Atlantic World in the First-Half of the Nineteenth Century (1806-1866)" by Claudia Schnurmann (mentioned in the note above) at www.immigrantentrepreneurship.org. Professor Schnurmann wrote to me that "Moritz Heckscher was born in 1797 and converted to the Protestant confession in 1808; his father reached that decision only in 1815. The lawyer acted as minister of foreign affairs in the short-lived Frankfurter Paulskirche only for a very short period of time (August-December 1848); it was the unsuccessful effort to create a German nation state but it took more years till the second German empire was created in 1870/71. See the cv of Heckscher in NDB 8, 1969 deutsche-biographie.de" The article has extensive footnotes (Zahara)

5   He apparently commissioned a genealogy of which I have a copy. This has been very useful to me in establishing our family tree. [This reference from Helmut is unclear. He does not state who commissioned it or where it is. It may be in the Helmut Heckscher files (Zahara).]

6   My father Max died of a stroke in Milwaukee, Wisconsin on March 22, 1963. (Helmut).

7   On our 1993 trip to Germany, I considered visiting Jauer, but couldn't find it on the map. The reason, which I only later discovered, was that Jauer is now in Poland and had been renamed Jaworze. It was too far out of our way to visit. (Helmut)

8   On my 1993 visit to Hamburg, I located the Kloepper building. I wanted to revisit the place where my father had spent much of his life. However, the building was under a new ownership and a guard at the front desk barred me from entering. (Helmut)

9   The information comes from documents in my file. However, in an autobiographical note, my father wrote that he had liquidated the cigar factory in 1915. (Helmut). Unfortunately, I have not been able to find the full note, just a short translation and summary by Helmut, included in the appendix. (Zahara)

10   The Pintus family had two sons. One died before WW II. The other, Ernst Pintus, escaped to London, where he lived to about age 90. His wife, although 30 years younger, pre-diseased him by several weeks. Sadly, Helmut thought Ernst, his first cousin, had passed away sooner, based on faulty research by a detective Helmut had hired. So although Helmut travelled to England many times, he never connected with Ernst there. The archivist of Hamburg was notified of Ernst's death in about 1993. By coincidence, the archivist knew Helmut, and notified him so Helmut received the bequest. Zahara and Helmut traveled to England and visited the house before it was sold. Zahara learned about Ernst from his neighbor. A note about the process of getting the bequest is in the Helmut Heckscher files. Helmut's other first cousin, from his mother's side, Rita Oshinsky (nee Goldstein), fled Germany in 1935 for what was then Palestine. In Palestine, she met and married Egon "Cushi" Oschinsky, an architect from Breslau. Rita's parents, Else "Meitz" Goldstein (nee Leipziger) and Richard Josef Goldstein, visited her there in 1937, but did not like it, and returned to Cottbus, Germany, not realizing the danger. There, Richard was thrown from a tram (because he was Jewish) and badly injured. In 1940, they fled the Nazis, once again heading for Palestine, this time via Bratislava. But the Italian steam paddler they took, the Pencho, had engine trouble and wrecked in the Dodecanese Islands. (See the book Odyssey by John Bierman.) The Italians placed them in the internment camp in Ferramonti. Richard died there in 1943. Else continued her journey to Palestine, arriving via Egypt on the day Rita'sdaughter Alisa Barkatt (nee Oschinsky) was born, June 5, 1944. Rita and Egon stayed in Palestine/Israel until their deaths in 1995 and 1996. Alisa moved with her husband Aaron "Roni" Barkatt to the US, setting in Maryland, where she reconnected with Zahara. These notes are from Alisa's communication with Zahara.

11   Perhaps Helmut meant to say she had hoped for a girl, which he had mentioned to me several times. In some of his baby pictures, he seems to be dressed as a girl, but that may have also been the custom at the time for all babies. (Zahara)

12   Zahara interviewed Helmut in 2008. The transcripts of the interview
      are in the Helmut Heckscher files, in a three ring blue binder, along
      with a disc of the transcript. Rachel may have the CD. In those
      document, Helmut adds some additional details about his early
      childhood, like having to eat a raw egg every day so he would grow
      taller. He includes other details of his later life, leaving Germany and
      being in the Army as well. The recordings do not seem to include life
      after marriage. (Zahara)

13   Later, when he lived in the United States, my father learned to drive
      and loved it with a passion. It was a tragedy when, in his 80's, he lost
      his driver's license because of a minor traffic violation. (Helmut)

14   Rachel and I visited Hamburg in 1993. As part of the trip we visited
      The Elbe River. (Helmut). Zahara joined this trip later, but missed
      the Elbe. David visited with Helmut and Margaret on a later trip.
      (Zahara)

15   The Oberstrasse Temple, built in 1931, was the third location of what
      was arguably the first Reform Jewish community in the world; the
      liberal Jews of Hamburg were on the forefront of the development
      of the Reform movement which later took hold in the United States.
      (Zahara)

16   Technically, the chair is meant to be for Elijah, not the Messiah. As
      he states, Helmut's religious education was spotty. He once surprised
      me, when he was about 75, by asking "Do Christians think Jesus
      was the Messiah." I answered "yes," somewhat amazed that he had
      reached such a ripe age without knowing that. Or maybe he once
      knew but had forgotten. (Zahara)

17   When Helmut first told me his family celebrated Christmas, I was
      quite surprised, but I later learned that assimilated Jews in Germany
      commonly celebrated Christmas, complete with trees and presents,
      as a sort of secular national holiday (Zahara).

18   I own an 800 page biography by Ron Chernow, called *The Warburgs*.
      The Warburgs were another German-Jewish family who had settled
      in Hamburg. Successful bankers, they probably rivaled only the
      Rothschilds. Chernow cites two quotes that seem pertinent to the fate
      of my parents and their friends. The quotes still apply to all Jews in
      the Diaspora, even those in America. The first, written long before
      the Holocaust, is by Jacob Wassermann, a novelist, in his *My Life as
      a German and a Jew*:

"The non-German cannot possibly imagine the heartbreaking position of the German Jew. 'German Jew' - you must place full emphasis on both words. You must understand them as the final product of a lengthy evolutionary process. His twofold love and his struggle on two fronts drive him close to despair."

Chernow, himself, writes:

"The German Jews were a people shipwrecked by history. Arguably the most productive group of Jews in history, they were also in many ways the least typical. Few groups have been so admired for their achievements, or so maligned for their attitudes. Persecuted by other Germans as too Jewish, they were often scorned by other Jews as too German. Their existence rested on a tenuous illusion of acceptance until the Nazis came along and tore that dream to tatters. People still puzzle over why these bright, industrious people were so blind to a mortal threat to their existence. In frustration, some Jews deny them the dignity of their tragedy."

Chernow means Jews who had not lived under Hitler.
(Helmut)

19 Letter is in the Hecksher files. (Zahara)
20 I remember that Helmut told me that a Danish farmer who let them stay at his barn later helped Dad get on the Kindertransport. I am not sure if I am remembering this correctly and I have not yet found evidence. (Zahara)
21 Though we were, of course, poles apart, I am now struck by certain similarities between the Hitler youth groups and our own. In both groups, youth revered those who had given their lives for a cause, and both groups taught that a Spartan life was better than a soft, indulgent one. Most importantly, both groups gave their members a sense of belonging that transcended the personal insecurities that teenagers, left to themselves, often experience (Helmut). Helmut's grandson, Max Heckscher, participates in a summer camp program, Camp Moshava, which has its roots in the same Habonim movement that Helmut was part of in his youth (Zahara).

22 A detailed account of this is given in *Kristallnacht: The Nazi Night of Terror*, by Anthony Read and David Fisher, Random House, 1989. (Helmut)

23 For some reason, perhaps because we visited Buchenwald in 1993, I thought that Helmut's father, Max Heckscher, had been sent to Buchenwald. But the Holocaust Museum website database confirms that he was sent to Sachsenhausen (Zahara).

24 This "Rosa Story" was written up in Time Magazine and later in Milwaukee newspapers. In these stories she is sometimes referred to as "Rose." The details differ slightly from Helmut's recollection. See appendix. (Zahara)

25 Menoti, in one of his short operas, "The Consul" dramatized the plight of refugees seeking asylum from persecution. (Helmut)

26 Zahara's friend Keith Shur, a WWII buff, notes that "What really did the Germans in was the British radar network that allowed the British to vector their smaller fighter force to intercept the German bomber streams while they were transiting the Channel. Also the German fighters had limited fuel range, so it was difficult for them to protect the bombers, especially over London. Finally, every German crew bailed out over England was lost vs. the British crew could potentially fight again." (Zahara)

27 See passenger list from November 16, 1940. (List or manifest of alien passengers). (Helmut). This may be in the Helmut heckscher files (Zahara).

28 One of the first lines of the Army song "You are in the Army Now" by Status Quo:

A vacation in a foreign land, Uncle Sam does the best he can
You're in the Army now, oh-oo-oh you're in the Army now

Now you remember what the draft man said,
nothing to do all day but stay in bed
You're in the Army now, oh-oo-oh you're in the Army now...

29 This section is funny for me to read, since I also attended the University of Wisconsin in Madison, and it was one of the worst years of my life – I despised the weather, the short days made me depressed,

I missed my community in DC, and I did not find any charm in Madison, except for the pleasure of studying with the pioneering African Historian Yan Vansina, and working as an assistant to a program with some comrades from the African National Congress. (Zahara)

30   It seems that Helmut never got around to writing about Berkeley. The fact that he was admitted to the Physics Department there (probably the top place in the world to study physics at that time) is a testament to his intelligence and hard work. But he once told me that he felt surrounded by so many geniuses at Berkeley that he thought he could not compete. So he transferred to study an easier topic, education, at a lesser place: Harvard! (Zahara)

31   Helmut's resume and information on his patents are in the Helmut Heckscher files. (Zahara)

32   See Kitty Tancock's biography of Bridget in the Appendix. (Zahara)

33   At present, spring 1995, I am giving a course on satire. (Helmut)

Printed in the United States
By Bookmasters